PHILANTHROPY
at Independent Schools

THIRD EDITION

Helen A. Colson, Editor

D1540402

NATIONAL ASSOCIATION OF INDEPENDENT SCHOOLS

ISBN: 1-893021-78-5
Printed in the United States of America

NATIONAL ASSOCIATION OF INDEPENDENT SCHOOLS

The National Association of Independent Schools represents approximately 1,400 independent private schools in the United States and other countries.
All are accredited, non-discriminatory, nonprofit organizations governed by independent boards of trustees. NAIS's mission is to serve and strengthen member schools and associations by "articulating and promoting high standards of education quality and ethical behavior; to work to preserve their independence to serve the free society from which that independence derives; to advocate broad access for students by affirming the principles of diversity, choice, and opportunity."

To find out more information, go to the NAIS website at *www.nais.org*. To receive a listing of NAIS books, call (800) 793-6701 or 240-646-7052.

Editors: Susan Hunt and Nancy Raley
Book Designer: Fletcher Design, Washington, DC

FSC
Mixed Sources
Product group from well-managed forests, controlled sources and recycled wood or fiber

Cert no. SW-COC-002062
www.fsc.org
© 1996 Forest Stewardship Council

CONTENTS

Introduction

It is a pleasure to share the third edition of NAIS's *Philanthropy at Independent Schools* with 15 co-authors who have contributed their expertise and talents to a significantly expanded book. Each of the chapters reflects the opinions of its author and not necessarily those of the other authors or of NAIS. The Reynolds School, which appears in several chapters, is a fictitious institution.

Since the first edition of this book was published 14 years ago, the world of independent school development has expanded and changed. This text reflects both the increased sophistication of development programs and the increased professionalism of those who guide them. It is my hope that the information and insights it offers will challenge readers to think about their own development agendas in new and creative ways.

Like so many with a zest for independent schools, I appreciate the innovation and energy of NAIS President Pat Bassett. I am also grateful to my longtime NAIS friends, Donna Orem and Jefferson Burnett, who answered questions and reviewed chapters. I thank Susan Hunt for her careful editing and, in particular, Nancy Raley, who skillfully and gracefully shepherded this book over many months from a first conversation to a final product.

Thanks also to Carol Cheney who reviewed several chapters in addition to her own, to Mary Carrasco and Michael Miller who contributed to the text, to Elizabeth Robelen who assisted with editing and proofreading, and to Earl Colson who offered valuable suggestions at every step of the way.

On behalf of my co-authors and myself, I applaud the philanthropists who are contributing critical resources to institutions increasingly dependent upon voluntary support and whose generosity affirms that independent education is essential to promoting innovation, leadership, and mutual respect in a changing world.

Notwithstanding economic uncertainties, the future of independent school philanthropy is bright. As both friend makers and fund raisers know, it is extraordinarily rewarding to bring together a generous donor and a worthy cause. The best development programs bring joy to all involved.

Helen A. Colson
Chevy Chase, Maryland
February 2009

21ST CENTURY
PHILANTHROPY

CHAPTER 1

Fund Raising in the 21st Century: Trends and Consequences

By Helen A. Colson

Independent schools in the 21st century have never had more to offer. Their curricula are creative; their environments are supportive; and their community spirit is strong.

Where else can one find a class small enough to provide individual attention but large enough to offer access, via the Internet, to knowledge throughout the world? Where else do teachers have the freedom to innovate? What better enriches the education of all students than a school community reflecting the social, ethnic, racial, religious, and economic diversity of the world in which its graduates will live?

Nevertheless, remaining excellent and competitive presents significant challenges to those responsible for what is variously referred to as "development," "advancement," and "external affairs." For development officers, school heads, fund-raising volunteers, and trustees, there are new fiscal needs to be met, new pressures to achieve high goals, and new constituencies and demographic groups to understand. Furthermore, an effective board of trustees has never been more important.

CHALLENGES FOR FUND RAISERS

During the 21st century, all independent schools will be more reliant on annual, capital, and planned giving revenue and on endowment income to ensure their financial sustainability. Schools will continue to achieve increased fund-raising goals because, although today's major donors are fewer in number, their gifts are larger in size. Annual funds of $1 million are no longer the exception. During capital campaigns, as much as 70 percent of the money comes from gifts of $1 million or more.

At the same time, there is more competition for voluntary support. The number of nonprofits is proliferating at a rapid rate, and donors are deluged with gift requests. In the education sector, public school foundations and charter schools have entered the fund-raising arena with professional programs and staff.

It is the smaller number of wealthier constituents (as distinguished from foundations and corporations) who are contributing 85 percent of the money raised by independent schools. Therefore, the best development programs are focused on those individual prospects who are in the top 10 percent of the pool in terms of their potential to give. The development staff should pay close attention to these top prospects' perspectives, objectives, interests, and timetables rather than simply to the institution's needs. School leaders should develop close personal relationships with top prospects and should be thoughtful stewards of previous gifts.

These 21st century donors who are, as a group, more affluent than in the past, are also more discriminating and demanding. They give to schools whose values they share, whose leadership they trust, whose budgets are stable, whose fiscal management is transparent, and whose strategic planning is bold. They appreciate creativity in fund raising and expect a careful evaluation of fund-raising results.

Given the fact that philanthropy is often a school's fastest growing income stream, it is an irony that many development programs are far too limited in resources and staffs. In the 21st century, well-funded programs and an adequate staff are essential if a school is to achieve its fund-raising potential. This is particularly true because volunteers from two-career families have less discretionary time, so schools must depend more than ever on their fund-raising staff.

THE EVER-INCREASING NEED

Even as schools offer more, they need more as well. As Patrick F. Bassett and Mark J. Mitchell observed in their 2006 NAIS publication, *Financing Sustainable Schools*, there are serious challenges to financial sustainability throughout the independent school world.

Among the most significant are the following:

- *Tuition increases*: Tuition continues to outpace inflation growth even though, at many schools, there has been little change in the percentage of students receiving financial aid.

- *Declining enrollment*: Enrollment is at best flat and, in some markets, is declining due to (a) demographic changes, (b) the financial concerns of middle class parents (many of whose incomes are not keeping pace with increased costs), and (c) increased choices, including better public and parochial schools, new charter schools, and home schooling.

- *Increased faculty and staff*: In recent decades, the average staff size has increased by one-third as schools respond to (a) the challenge of program innovation to prepare students for the 21st century marketplace, (b) the expanded role of technology, and (c) a growing awareness and sensitivity to different learning styles.

- *Retiring and scarce teachers*: Schools are hiring an unprecedented number of new teachers to replace a large cohort of retiring teachers. At the same time, there are fewer new teachers who wish to and can afford to make teaching a lifelong career. This is bidding up salaries and employer contributions to retirement and benefit plans.

- *Overextension of debt*: To build new facilities and to maintain existing plants — and because of the availability of tax-free bonds — many schools are taking on vastly increased levels of debt.

- *New concerns about security*: Schools are increasingly aware of the potential consequences of societal unrest and economic downturns and of the need for security. Trustees and administrators know that they need ample savings, just as an individual does, for unanticipated emergencies and in unpredictable times.

These challenges create increased pressure on the school's fund-raising staff. On the one hand, charitable giving in general and to educational institutions in particular has increased each year, albeit more slowly in recent times. On the other hand, at many schools, giving goals are based unrealistically on institutional need rather than on fund-raising potential.

THE 21st CENTURY PROSPECT: A DEMOGRAPHIC MIX

There has never been one single way to approach a major gift prospect. To the contrary, successful major gift philanthropy has always been geared to the differences between individual donors.

However, in the 21st century, there is increasing awareness that the age of the prospective donor has a significant impact on his or her philanthropic values and preferences. Wise development professionals are shaping their fund-raising approaches and messages to appeal to distinct demographic groups who see the world quite differently.

Within schools today, there are several different and distinct generations:

- *The Silent Generation and War Babies*: grandparents, parents, parents of alumni, and, in some cases, alumni who were born before 1945. As a group, they are more formal and more disciplined. They value loyalty and service.

- *Baby Boomers*: the largest population group, born between 1946 and 1964, and encompassing all constituencies — parents, parents of alumni, alumni, and grandparents. They have a strong work ethic and value career success, teamwork, and consensus building. They see their children as the school's customers.

- *Generation Xers*: parents and alumni of the present and future, born between 1965 and 1978. They are defined by their lifestyle rather than by their jobs. They are entrepreneurial and value individuality and creativity. They appreciate immediate results and wish to communicate instantly. They see themselves as the school's customers.

- *Millennials*: young parents, alumni, and future alumni born after 1979. They are steeped in technology, and they value community and diversity. They are brand-conscious, optimistic, impatient, and focused on achievement.

The Baby Boomers, who have been the bedrock of independent school philanthropy in the past, are now benefiting from the largest intergenerational transfer of wealth in history. To increase their past gift levels, they must be offered the opportunity to make tax-wise planned gifts in order to combine both outright and deferred support.

The Generation Xers and Millennials are emerging as a new and distinct pool that will shape philanthropy for years to come. Therefore, it is important to examine their characteristics and preferences more closely.

Previous generations of philanthropists have said, "Mr. Headmaster, please accept my gift and use it as you think best." These new 21st century donors are more likely to say, "Here is my gift. I view it as an investment in your school, and I want you to keep me informed about the quality and nature of the return."

Here's what these Generation Xers and Millennials seek and what schools should provide:

1. *Engagement* in the life of the school so that philanthropic support adds value to the donor's life as well as to the life of the school. They want to help solve problems, work on creative future plans, and provide expertise as well as financial resources.

2. *Quick, efficient service*, including immediate access on the web to up-to-date information about the school's strategic plans, finances, fundraising campaigns, and progress toward meeting its goals.

3. *Education* about the school's distinct mission, why tuition is so high, why education is so expensive, why (unlike the profit sector) customers pay less than the full cost, how much it costs to raise a dollar, and how their gifts will have a clear and positive impact on the school.

4. *Confidence* that the school's finances are well planned and well managed, that the administration and trustees are good stewards of the school's resources, and that their gifts are leading to meaningful, measurable, and positive change.

Fund raisers should be aware of the business mentality that many of these donors (often called "venture philanthropists") apply to the nonprofit world. Development directors should design major gift programs that are as distinct, clear, competitive, and appealing as the best commercial brands.

In short, the development director of today must be steeped in the ethos and culture of these important demographic groups, and he or she must understand their styles and preferences as well.

AGING DONORS, WOMEN PHILANTHROPISTS, AND PARENTS NEW TO INDEPENDENT SCHOOLS

There are also three constituency groups that deserve the development director's close attention. They are aging donors, women philanthropists, and parents new to independent schools.

By the year 2050, it is projected that one in five Americans will be over age 65.[1] These may be as many as 20 percent of a school's potential donors as well. As a result, planned giving will continue to play an essential role in independent school development, particularly in endowment fund raising.

In the 21st century, every independent school, new and old, small and large, must have a planned giving program. Furthermore, development professionals must focus research and cultivation efforts on older alumni and grandparents. They must find new ways to involve older prospects in the life of the school and new ways to educate them about tax-wise giving opportunities. (See Chapter 8.)

Women donors, now in a position of unprecedented earned wealth and economic power, also are playing an increasingly important role in philanthropy. Because women outlive men by an average of seven years, many are the beneficiaries of many trillions of dollars of inherited wealth, which is now being transferred from one generation to the next.

Many women are introduced to philanthropy as volunteers. As donors, they want a partnership with the school; they value face-to-face contact. They should be individually cultivated and appreciated for their colleagueship and commitment as well as for their gifts.

Finally, development professionals should look carefully at parents new to independent schools.

There was a time when the majority of parents understood the need for

---

[1] U.S. Census Bureau, 2004, "U.S. Interim Projections by Age, Sex, Race, and Hispanic Origin," online at *http://www.census.gov/ipc/www/usinterimproj/*.

voluntary support. Many were independent school alumni and habitual do-nors; some became significant philanthropists as well. That time has passed. Today's parents reflect both the pluralism of the population nationwide and a determined effort on the part of schools to become more culturally, racially, religiously, and economically diverse.

These parents may not understand the need for or the role of voluntary support. They may not understand the economics of private-sector educa-tion. If they attended public schools, they may believe that their school, which charges a high tuition, is rich, that its fiscal reserves are large, and that its teachers are well paid. If they have immigrated from abroad or are sending their children to boarding schools from Europe, the Middle East, South America, or the Pacific Rim, they may feel that they have a business relationship with the school from which they are purchasing a service at its market value.

To transform these parents into philanthropists takes a carefully planned curriculum that focuses on the role of the nonprofit sector, the mission of the school, the economics of independent education, and the school's need for voluntary support.

Many development professionals do not realize that the prominence and stature of the nonprofit sector is a largely American phenomenon. In parts of the world from which increasing numbers of independent school students come, there is little tradition of philanthropy as it is understood in the United States.

Therefore, for some parents, the fund-raising education should begin with Philanthropy 101: the importance of the independent sector and the role it plays in promoting choice, innovation, and excellence. These par-ents should be taught that philanthropy (voluntary action for public good) is invaluable in a democratic society and key to excellence at independent schools.

In addition, parents unfamiliar with independent school education may not understand these schools' deep commitment to a value-centered educa-tion that not only prepares students for college but also teaches them to re-spect those who think differently and inspires them to help those who have been given less.

The institutional mission — to teach students to live fully and productively in a complex world with shrinking resources — is an important aspect of the fund-raising appeal. For many parents new to independent schools, it is the school's noble mission that makes it worthy of philanthropic support.

Finally, these parents have something important in common with all of the groups described above: They must be educated about the economics of independent school education, the financial constraints of their particular school, and its need for and uses of voluntary support. This education, which makes the case for the institution rather than just for a particular campaign, should precede the school's annual giving appeal, and it should be delivered in person to those with the potential to make major gifts.

THE CRITICAL IMPORTANCE OF TRUSTEESHIP

To meet the challenges of the 21st century, independent schools have to rely more than ever before on enlightened trusteeship. At the same time, there is a preponderance of inexperienced trustees, unfamiliar with the role of the board and with their individual responsibilities.

It is critically important that schools seek board members who are intelligent and thoughtful, who care deeply about the school, who understand the distinction between *setting* policy (which they do) and *implementing* policy (which the school head does), and who can bring sound judgment and skills to governance.

To find and to interest such trustees, the Committee on Trustees (also known as the Governance Committee) should pay close attention to the recruitment and orientation of new trustees. In particular, the committee members should be responsible for the following:

- Vigorously and continuously cultivating potential trustees
- Providing a clearly written job description for all trustees (see box on page 14)
- Formally orienting new trustees
- Asking all trustees to evaluate their service once a year
- Renominating trustees only when it is deserved

From a development perspective, trustees have significant fiduciary and fund-raising roles. Their *fiduciary* responsibilities include the following:

1. *Ensuring institutional readiness* by providing a compelling mission statement, keeping strategic plans up-to-date, describing present and future facility needs and costs clearly, setting short- and long-term endowment goals, and educating the community about the need for philanthropy

2. *Ensuring fund-raising readiness* by requiring and reviewing an annual development plan, providing funds to compensate an experienced and competent development staff, asking the school head to make fund raising one of his or her priorities, and establishing clear gift acceptance and crediting policies

Their *fund-raising* responsibilities include the following:

1. Making the school a personal philanthropic priority

2. Helping identify and evaluate major prospects

3. Cultivating and stewarding major prospects on an individual basis

4. Soliciting major prospects as appropriate

5. Monitoring and evaluating fund-raising progress

New trustees often ask, "What does philanthropic priority mean?" At independent schools, it refers to the nature of the gift rather than the amount. Trustees typically are asked to make the school one of their top charitable causes during their service on the board. On an economically diverse board, this amount may vary significantly from one trustee to another. It is not unusual for a trustee to make a $10,000 pledge more sacrificially than another who pledges $500,000. On the other hand, it is important to have some major gift prospects on the board to set a high standard of support for others in the community who have the ability to follow their lead.

Should all trustees be required to solicit gifts? At most schools, the answer is "no." However, those board members who initially are reluctant to ask for voluntary support often feel more comfortable after they attend a solicitor training session and accompany a fellow trustee on a solicitation call.

FUND RAISING IN UNCERTAIN TIMES

According to the Giving USA Foundation, total giving to nonprofit institutions has increased, in constant dollars, every year since 1955 with the exception of 1987 (when a tax law change the previous year prompted some donors to give early).

This was true during the stock market declines of the 1970s and during the dramatic October and November decline in 1987. It has been true in the 1990s and since 2000 as well.

However, in the 21st century, there is growing uncertainty about what the future will bring. How should that affect fund-raising plans? It is wise to follow these guidelines:

- Do not put a campaign on hold because of economic conditions. Most other schools in particular and nonprofits in general will be going ahead with campaigns. Schools that delay will lose their competitive positions.

- Do focus on top prospects — those who often are giving to charitable organizations way below their potential.

- Be prepared to discuss major gifts one year at a time. Put a five-year capital campaign pledge aside when asked to do so and instead ask for commitments year by year.

- Stress the particular need as families and faculty struggle with unanticipated financial concerns. "We have never needed your support more than we do now."

- Acknowledge the particular commitment of generous donors. "We understand that the very reasons that make our need so urgent also have an impact on you and your family."

- Continue to set ambitious goals, but test them carefully before they are publicly announced.

- Don't overlook planned gift options that permit donors to leverage their support with combined outright and deferred gifts.

Every trustee, school head, and development professional should remember that, even when market forces are uncertain, there still are economic benefits to giving. In particular, there are three enduring concepts related to the tax advantages of a gift:

1. If a donor is in a top income tax bracket, a charitable gift will cost considerably less when federal and state income tax charitable deductions are taken into account.

2. Many potential donors own appreciated securities held for more than one year, which, if they are given to the school, permit the donor to (a) take an income tax deduction for the appreciated value and (b) avoid a capital gains tax.

3. Even the sale of depreciated securities, without regard to how long they have been held, permits the donor to (a) take an income tax deduction for the cash gift and (b) take a capital loss that can be used to offset current and future capital gains.

Independent school development programs will continue to thrive during the ups and downs of the economy and notwithstanding societal unrest if they are planned and implemented carefully and professionally. In fact, the danger of low expectations may be just as great as the danger of lower voluntary support.

THE JOY OF GIVING

Top donors to independent schools frequently say that giving to a worthy cause is a joy and that the job of fund raising is a pleasure. They view philanthropy as helping a school they treasure meet important ambitious goals. For many who have achieved success in life, the opportunity to give back brings satisfaction that cannot be realized in any other way.

Since so many of today's donors are looking for ways to add value to their lives, it is the wise school that focuses gift requests on the emotional return to those who empower present and future successes as well as on its need to achieve certain fund-raising goals.

TEN RESPONSIBILITIES
of an Independent School Trustee

1. To participate actively and regularly in board meetings and on board committees

2. To set policy for the school and to take action on budgetary and fiscal proposals

3. To perpetuate the school's mission and values

4. To make the school a personal philanthropic priority during the period of trusteeship

5. To make early contributions to annual and capital fund drives in order to motivate and to raise the sights of subsequent donors

6. To participate in donor cultivation activities and to solicit contributions with the guidance of the development office

7. To serve as an advocate of the school in the wider community

8. To recommend the school, as appropriate, to prospective students, teachers, and other employees

9. To avoid conflict of interest and the appearance of conflict of interest in all activities on behalf of the school

10. To participate in an annual trustee self-evaluation and an annual evaluation of the board as a whole

TEN PRINCIPLES
of Fund-Raising Excellence

Given the 21st century donor's call for transparent and responsible fiscal management and fund raising, schools should set and publicize the following principles that reflect both the best values of independent education and the highest standards of fund raising.

1. Purpose
The school will use all gifts only for the purposes for which they are sought or given.

2. Confidentiality
The school will offer all donors the opportunity to make anonymous gifts. It will also hold all research data regarding prospective donors in confidence.

3. Disclosure
The school will disclose annually the total amount of voluntary support it receives, the costs associated with the raising of those funds, and the uses to which the funds have been or will be put.

4. Leadership
The school will inform all donors of the names of those serving on the school's board of trustees, those in fund-raising leadership positions, and those in the top administration of the school.

5. Substitutions
The school will accept all gifts as voluntary contributions only, not in lieu of tuition or other fees.

6. Consultations
The school will encourage donors contemplating planned or deferred gifts to consult with their own attorneys or financial advisors during the decision-making process.

7. Information
The school will offer all donors access to its most recent financial statements and to other relevant public information.

8. Appreciation
The school will give all donors immediate acknowledgment of and appropriate recognition for their gifts.

9. Compensation
The school will hire development staff members and consultants only at prearranged set salaries or fees, which will not be contingent on fund-raising results.

10. Independence
The school reserves the right to refuse gifts that detract in any way from its character, integrity, or mission.

CHAPTER 2

The Plan, the Professional, and the Partnership

By Helen A. Colson

Effective development professionals make plans. They set priorities and goals. They prepare budgets and track expenses. They understand the relationship between the resources they have (staff, space, information systems, money, etc.) and the fund-raising results they are likely to achieve. They track cost-effectiveness — the relationship between money spent and money raised.

Schools whose development programs are guided by concise, clear, written plans are most likely to fulfill their fund-raising potential. Furthermore, schools whose development directors think ahead are better able to anticipate and manage change.

All professional development programs are based on two important resources: the school's mission statement and its strategic plan.

The mission statement tells what the school is trying to do, why, and for whom. It sets the tone of the fund-raising effort; it educates and cultivates potential donors. The mission statement should be communicated to all constituents and displayed prominently on the website and in the school. It should be reviewed regularly by the board of trustees as well as the faculty and staff.

The strategic plan tells how the school plans to implement its mis-

sion during the next three to five years. It identifies institutional priorities
and goals.

THE DEVELOPMENT PLAN

Most schools have development calendars. However, a calendar is only part
of a plan. The calendar tells when something will be done and often by
whom. The plan outlines why and how something will be done and with
what intended results. It identifies tasks, responsibilities, and timelines for all
aspects of the program.

The best development plans also acknowledge that fund-raising programs are least cost-effective at the start. As in most endeavors, an initial
investment is required to begin.

Many development directors — particularly those in small shops —
question whether planning is worth the effort and time. Ironically, they are
the professionals who most need a plan to move forward in these significant
ways:

1. *The development plan helps set realistic fund-raising goals.* Unrealistic
   goals are based on institutional needs alone. Realistic goals are based
   on fund-raising potential as well. They take into account the various
   resources a school can bring to bear: people, money, systems, and
   time. They acknowledge the level of staff experience and expertise.

2. *It helps set program priorities.* Development directors receive urgent requests from many fronts. However, only so many program initiatives
   are feasible in any one school year. Development directors who have
   set program priorities are able to focus on the most important work.

3. *It keeps staff and volunteers on schedule.* To achieve an annual giving
   goal by the end of June, one must take certain steps each month.
   All development activities — from a small class reunion to a major
   capital campaign — are geared to a series of deadlines that should be
   spelled out in advance.

4. *It helps the director delegate tasks.* A development plan leads to more
   effective delegation to both staff and volunteers. It encourages staff
   members to assume more personal responsibility for their work be-

cause they better understand that the development director cannot manage it all.

5. *It clarifies fiscal needs and keeps programs cost-effective.* Development planning includes a careful look at the resources spent and the money raised. It helps the staff keep track of costs and relate them to results. It focuses attention on percentages of growth by program and constituency from year to year. Often, the planning process helps the development director make an effective case for getting a bigger budget and a larger staff.

6. *It helps ensure a fair evaluation of program and staff.* When the board, the school head, and the development director agree on goals and priorities in advance, a year-end evaluation is likely to be more productive, useful, and fair.

7. *It educates key administrators and involves key prospects and volunteers.* Participation in planning leads to a proprietary interest in results. The more fully the school head and board understand the development challenges, the more helpful and supportive they will be. The same is true of fund-raising volunteers. The more major prospects are involved in the planning process, the better they will understand the urgency of the need and the importance of their generous support.

8. *It ensures that the program will become more professional each year.* Too many independent school development programs maintain the same level of professionalism each year. They may raise slightly more money, but they do not increase their sophistication or scope. Development planning forces a look at fund-raising concepts and techniques as well as fund-raising results. It is geared to tomorrow as well as to today.

THE PLANNING PROCESS AND TIMETABLE

Development planning is a team effort led by the development director, school head, and development committee chair. Among the planners are staff and volunteers who will be responsible for implementing the plan, key volunteers who will solicit gifts, and major prospects who have the ability to help the school achieve its fund-raising goals.

Many development professionals begin in January to plan for the following school year. As a result, they are well positioned to recommend or to react to an annual giving goal before it becomes a line item in the next year's budget. In the spring, the planners set fund-raising priorities, goals, and deadlines for the upcoming school year. In July, the staff makes adjustments based on a careful analysis of the previous year's fund-raising results. All of this helps the development office guard against the following:

- *Overscheduling*: planning too many mailings and events in any one month or asking the school head to do too much during January, February, and March, which are often his or her busiest times of the year

- *Poor timing*: scheduling a fund-raising event during the same week the annual appeal is mailed or sending an annual giving reminder on the day the second semester bill is mailed

Furthermore, planning makes it possible for the summer to be productive. The staff members can recruit and educate annual giving chairs and committees. They can prepare annual giving brochures. They can compose annual giving letters, even those to be mailed many months hence. As a result, in September, the annual giving program can focus on people rather than on paper, on individual leadership prospects rather than on constituency-wide appeals. During the school year, the staff and volunteers have time to cultivate top prospects, to create strategies for individual gift requests, and to evaluate progress along the way.

SPECIFIC GOALS

Often, a development plan highlights three or four specific areas for growth. For example, in a particular year, a school may aim to accomplish these goals:

Raise donor sights through leadership giving.

- Solicit all remaining capital campaign leadership prospects.

- Ask all previous annual giving donors in the leadership category for increased gifts.

- Add 50 donors to the top annual giving gift club.

Broaden the donor base.

- Increase the annual giving donor pool by 10 percent.

- Increase alumni participation in the annual fund to 35 percent.

- Increase parent participation in the annual fund to 85 percent.

- Successfully seek gifts from 100 LYBUNTs (donors who gave "Last Year But Unfortunately Not This" year) and SYBUNTs (those who gave "Some Years But Unfortunately Not This" year).

Provide high-quality major donor cultivation and stewardship activities.

- Select 75 prospects for ongoing person-to-person cultivation and track progress monthly.

- Organize weekly head of school breakfasts or lunches with top prospects and previous donors.

- Send letters to each capital campaign donor of $25,000 or above on the anniversary of his or her pledge or gift, expressing appreciation and describing the impact of the gifts.

- Host four regional reunions for alumni, parents of alumni, and grandparents.

THE DEVELOPMENT DIRECTOR

All of these activities are led by the development director, a key member of the school's senior administrative team.

Some development directors remain at the same school for 10 to 30 years. They are most likely to stay when they and their school heads share common values, similar ideals, and a commitment to fund-raising success. However, during the last decade, on average, school heads have searched for new development directors every two to four years. In an enterprise like development, which depends on building personal relationships, this is an alarming trend.

Why don't they stay longer? Several reasons stand out:

1. *A poor fit.* Just as the right chemistry between the school head and the development director makes fund-raising success possible, the wrong

chemistry undermines effectiveness and makes the fund raiser dissatisfied with the job.

2. *Compensation.* Development directors' salaries have increased more slowly at independent schools than elsewhere in the nonprofit world. Often, skilled development professionals can earn more at another job.

3. *A wider choice.* More nonprofit organizations are hiring development officers every year. Opportunities for skilled, experienced professionals abound.

4. *Burnout.* Even the best development director cannot meet every institutional need; schools must set priorities. But some heads, trustees, and fund-raising volunteers have unrealistic expectations about what a fund raiser can accomplish in a single school year. Their development directors try to please, but after a few years, they burn out.

THE IDEAL CANDIDATE

There is no one profile for the ideal candidate. To the contrary, top-notch independent school development directors often have dissimilar resumes. Their educations are diverse; few took fund-raising courses in school. Their work experiences are varied; few focused on development from the start of their careers.

Some come on board with in-depth knowledge of their schools, perhaps because they are alumni, parents, or current employees. Others have development expertise but must learn about the institutions they serve.

As in all jobs, relevant experience counts. A candidate who has managed annual and capital drives at a school has particular appeal. However, equally important are several characteristics that the best development directors share:

1. *Creativity.* Talented development directors have initiative and a zest for new ideas. They focus first on fund-raising concepts (what are we trying to accomplish and why?) and only thereafter on fund-raising techniques (how are we going to do it and when?).

2. *Flexibility.* All development directors have a multi-faceted job that re-

quires working with a variety of people. They must interact patiently and successfully with colleagues, trustees, and volunteer leaders.

3. *Communication skills.* Successful development directors communicate confidently and well, often with constituents from diverse cultures. They speak effectively and persuasively. They write quickly and with ease.

4. *Eagerness to learn.* There are few college degrees in development, but there are many opportunities to learn. The best development directors continue to learn throughout their careers. They seek opportunities and set aside time for professional growth.

5. *A passion for detail.* In development, success or failure is often in the details. Records must be accurate; names must be correct; gift acknowledgments must be prompt. The best development directors are computer-literate, careful, and consistent.

6. *The ability to lead.* Good development directors enjoy a leadership role and know how to build consensus. Staff members are happy to be on their teams.

7. *The ability to follow.* Development directors must also follow the lead of the head of school. The most successful development professionals understand the head of school's objectives and priorities and represent them well at all times.

CONDUCTING THE SEARCH

Because networking is often the best way to find appropriate and experienced candidates, most school heads begin a search by consulting their peers. Next, they place advertisements in local and national fund-raising newsletters, on online job banks, in local newspapers, and in *The Chronicle of Philanthropy*. Although ads can be expensive, they do cast a wide net — one that can be very important to school heads with only a short time to fill a key job. Some schools use search firms.

Once applications arrive and three to five top candidates emerge, the next step is to interview with care. Although it is the school head who has the final say about a new development director, most heads ask others, for example, the board chair, the capital campaign chair, the business manager, and a few key volunteers, to help assess candidates during school visits. Finalists should also meet with every member of the development office staff.

Too often, schools rush through the last important step: meticulous reference checks. Conversations with those who know the candidates should be probing, candid, and clear. The reference checkers should ask each person whose name the applicant provides to give the name of someone else who can also evaluate the candidate. Failing to check thoroughly may lead to a poor choice for the school.

THE SCHOOL HEAD-DEVELOPMENT DIRECTOR PARTNERSHIP

Hiring the right development director is only the start; thereafter, the head of school should empower the development director and support the program he or she leads.

It is up to the head of school to give fund raising high visibility and the fund-raising professional high credibility within the school. And it is up to the head of school to encourage and to facilitate the development director's interaction with trustees, alumni, parents, prospects, volunteers, faculty, and staff.

Most important, the head of school and the development director should work together in a mutually supportive manner. There are seven ways in which the school head can make the important relationship with his or her development director thrive:

1. Schedule a regular weekly meeting with the development director.

2. Agree with the development director about the 10 priorities for each school year and rank them in order of importance.

3. Invite the development director to attend meetings of the board of trustees and of the board's development, finance, and governance committees.

4. Include reports by the development director at faculty meetings several times a year.

5. Offer the development director opportunities to attend workshops and conferences to ensure his or her professional growth.

6. Let the development director manage his or her time. Don't load him or her up with lunchroom duties or responsibilities for the carpool line.

7. Make it clear that the development director is a key and trusted member of the senior administration.

In return, the development director might pledge to do the following:

1. Respect the school head's busy schedule and try to use his or her fund-raising time wisely and well.

2. Prepare the school head fully, both orally and with written memoranda, for meetings with major prospects and key fund-raising groups.

3. Manage the development staff and budget with skill.

4. Work cooperatively with fellow administrators and be sensitive and responsive to their differing points of view.

5. Have a passion for the school, be inspired by its mission, and consider it a privilege to advance its goals.

The development director knows better than anyone else the importance of thanks. He or she is the one who makes sure that donors and volunteers get frequent and fulsome praise. Therefore, it is the wise school head who remembers that the development director deserves, needs, and values thanks as well. Ample appreciation from the boss goes a very long way.

FUND-RAISING RESULTS
How Much and Compared with Whom?

"I just received an annual report from my other child's school. Why does it raise so much more money than we do?"

Sometimes comparing one school's fund-raising results with another's is appropriate, but often it is not. Two schools in the same city and of similar size may achieve significantly different fund-raising results. One, for example, may have alumni who are older, who are more numerous, and who have multigenerational ties. One school's parents may be more accustomed to philanthropy, and the trustees' development roles may be better defined. Furthermore, its development program may be well-established and more generously funded and its staff larger and better trained.

When fund-raising comparisons are made with other schools, they should be on the basis of funds raised per student and improved results from year to year, rather than on the basis of total funds raised in a particular year. Via its Stats-Online service, NAIS offers its members the ability to access these data and to develop customized reports that permit schools to compare themselves with selected institutions and in appropriate ways. (For more about StatsOnline, visit *www.nais.org*.)

In addition, the national summaries by NAIS and the Council for Aid to Education are helpful in identifying averages, ranges, and trends. However, it is not fair to use them in isolation to make a particular development office (or professional) look good (or bad). There are simply too many other factors at play.

The most useful comparisons of fund-raising results are with past performance at one's own school. Development directors should ask themselves these questions every year:

1. Is the annual fund producing more money each year and an increased percentage of the school's operating revenue?
2. Is the program adding significantly to the donor pool?
3. Has the average annual gift increased?
4. Is effective research increasing the prospect pool?
5. Is sufficient attention focused on major prospects and major gifts?
6. Is too much time or money being spent relative to the amount raised?

CHAPTER 3

International Schools: New Frontiers in Fund Raising

By Carrie Levenson-Wahl

In order to understand the challenges of fund raising in an international school setting, picture the following situation:

A new director of development arrives at a school that has never had a history of raising money. More than half the population of the school does not speak English as a first language, and there are over 50 different nationalities. In particular:

- There are no alumni records, no database of gift receipts, no events, no parent volunteers, no publications, and no culture of asking or giving.

- The head of school and the business manager think that revenue beyond tuition is unnecessary.

- The trustees are not accustomed to making or seeking charitable gifts.

- The faculty and staff resent the hiring of a development officer; they believe there are more pressing needs within their own departments.

- The school families typically stay for only one to three years, and often they receive no tax advantages when they make a charitable gift.

CULTURAL AND HISTORICAL CONTEXTS

A little background is helpful in order to appreciate the depth of this scenario.

The growth in international schools began in the early 1960s to meet the demands of global, mobile families. These families wanted an educational system for their children who moved to a new school in a new city every one to three years.

Because a family's successful relocation depended on the well-being and continued high-quality education of their children, the corporations and governments for whom these families worked provided most of the funding for these international schools. The availability of an appropriate school was often more important than housing or other ex-pat benefits. This funding pattern remains true to this day.

Today, there are well over 2,500 such schools in more than 100 countries. Many of them offer both the International Baccalaureate (IB) diploma and Advanced Placement (AP) programs, giving graduates the opportunity to apply to colleges and universities worldwide. About 75 to 80 percent of students attending many international schools have their tuition and other costs underwritten by multinational corporations, embassies, or UN organizations, thereby fostering the impression that international schools do not need extra funding and that dependency on big corporations and government agencies is more than sufficient.

Philanthropy in Europe also has a particular historical context. While Europeans are certainly philanthropic, schools are not perceived as charitable entities. In much of Europe, no one worries about the costs of schooling because governments pay for education at the primary, secondary, and university levels. Private schools are viewed as elitist and expensive, while international schools, at which the instruction is in English, are often looked upon with distrust or indifference. They are all perceived as being "rich" and not in need of extra funds.

Fund raising in international schools came into its own in the mid- to late 1990s and first took hold in the United Kingdom. It followed the tried-and-true American principles, first developing a strong annual fund, then moving into a capital campaign, and finally building a major gifts program and an endowment. However, schools in other parts of Europe found that in order to prove that raising money was even possible, it was necessary to begin with a major gifts initiative and then "back into" an annual fund. While counterintuitive, this method did work. New buildings went up, theaters were fitted, and gyms were expanded. These initial efforts proved the value of having a full-time development director and helped orient trustees to the opportunity to seek charitable support. It also served to train and to give confidence to heads of school and to demonstrate that raising funds can be both lucrative and enjoyable.

INTERNATIONAL CHANGES AND CHALLENGES

However, it soon became apparent that a "quick-and-dirty" capital effort did not create enduring advancement programs. Because international schools have challenges that are particular to the way in which they are structured and to their individual missions, longer-term models were needed.

The international school development staff must tailor its appeals to the culture of the diverse national groups within its communities. For example, the Japanese sometimes give as a group and donate no more than the amount given by the highest-ranking member of their community. The French often find talking about money distasteful — something that one never mentions in conversation.

An obvious challenge in a European environment is one of language. Although the language of instruction in international schools is English, often the cultivation and asking are not. These schools often ask fellow nationals to educate and to solicit parents within their communities and to translate annual and capital fund materials into appropriate languages. The schools choose development directors not only because they are proven professionals but also because they are fluent in the language of the country in which they work. Working in a foreign country means speaking to printers, designers, event planners, and one's own administrative assistants in the host language. Cultivation and solicitation must take place in the language spoken by the prospective donor or head of the company. In France, this is particularly true. Being asked for a gift in French puts native speakers at ease and gives credibility to both the project and the solicitation.

Alumni programs in these schools present other fund-raising challenges.

Because they live literally all over the world, international school alumni rely on accurate databases and more advanced communication technology to remain in touch with their high schools and their high school friends. Many of these alumni attend more than one or two institutions during their school years, thus making it paramount for each school to capture and to keep their attention by providing current information, appealing websites, creative blogs, and easy-to-access alumni web pages.

Reunions must take place regularly, not just at the school and in cities within the United States but also in Paris, London, Tokyo, or Melbourne. In recent years, several European schools have united to host larger annual reunions in major cities, thus bringing together more than 300 alumni, alumni parents, and former teachers and sharing some of the cost. As more alumni reconnect with their alma maters and appreciate the efforts that development offices are making to reach out to them, they will begin to give back. However, it will take ongoing education to remind these former students that the corporate money that covered their tuitions in the past will no longer suffice for the current and future generations.

Another challenge unique to international schools is the high turnover of the current families. How can parents or alumni go through the traditional cycle of cultivation, solicitation, and stewardship in just one, two, or three years at the school? This is perhaps one of the most frustrating elements of fund raising within a European context. Welcoming new parents with one hand while soliciting them with the other goes against all professional and personal mores. It will remain difficult until a culture of philanthropy is established in international schools and donating becomes a habit as families move from one school to another. Nonetheless, the pioneering spirit of some advancement officers has given them the courage, when appropriate, to ask parents for a six-figure gift after only six months in the school!

U.S. citizens receive generous tax benefits for charitable giving in the United States. In Europe, where taxes are much higher, this is not always the case.

- In Belgium, there are no tax incentives.
- In Switzerland and France, schools, like other nonprofits, are not allowed to advertise. In Switzerland, this once even included putting

corporate names on plaques, but this is now allowed.

- In France, having an endowment was once considered tantamount to "earning money," which jeopardized a school's nonprofit status. France now offers significant tax benefits to both individuals and corporations, but these benefits are not well advertised and most often do not provide an incentive for making a donation.

Notwithstanding the fact that, as noted above, some of the restrictions have been lifted, due in no small part to lobbying by international schools, the perception still remains that giving to schools will not provide tax benefits to donors.

Because the challenge to increase voluntary support has become more urgent in recent years, many international schools also have sought and obtained a 501(c)(3) status in the United States so that their American families can have access to tax-deductible giving. The new urgency is due to the fact that many of the larger corporations and multinational companies, which have been paying not only the tuition fees but also the housing and health packages for their employees, are changing their policies. Some are cutting by half the amount they will pay for tuition. This significant reduction in the revenue on which most international schools depend is spurring boards and heads to consider more seriously other sources of income and to add a fund-raising component to their strategic plans.

Nevertheless, corporate support remains much more important to international schools than to schools in the states. Because of the implicit symbiotic relationship between these companies and the families who attend European schools, it is a natural quid pro quo association. International schools were founded to cater to global families and to create a seamless transition for students going back home or to another international school. Therefore, corporate gifts, as distinguished from tuition payments, are often quite large and, in many instances, go beyond the size of gifts received from individuals.

A more subtle, but nonetheless real, challenge for those working in this environment is the added burden on the development director. Working in one- to three-person shops, in charge of marketing, public relations, alumni relations, communications, events management, and fund raising, the development professional is under daily pressure to prove the value of the position and the department. Because of their lack of experience with fund raising, the board, the head of school, and the business manager may place unrealistic demands on the development director. Because they do not understand either the costs of starting an office or the time and skills it takes to establish a program, heads of schools often expect instant results, while boards create capital projects with improbable goals. Business managers, interested only in the bottom line, may add to the pressure by preferring to raise funds only for the immediate needs of the school, ignoring the importance of long-term development programming and goals. To be successful, the international school development director should have solid prior experience in the field, a strong and positive personality, perseverance, and patience.

TRENDS

There are some positive trends that are making fund raising in an international environment more attainable. Host country parents are looking at international schools as new and interesting alternatives. They may be dissatisfied with their own educational system and want an English language environment for their children, as well as the opportunities that an IB diploma or AP classes would afford them, or easier access to an American university. This has a stabilizing effect on the school, because these families are likely to have a longer tenure. In Paris, for example, many French parents are so grateful for the ambiance and welcoming component of their new school that they are beginning to make spontaneous and sometimes quite large charitable donations.

In addition, some families who initially moved abroad for one year (many among them simply because they "wanted to spend a year in _____") are so taken with the school and the lifestyle that they remain for a longer period. These are generally Americans who can afford to take this time off, who have disposable income, and who are used to giving. These families, then, become natural and easy donors. They bring with them the culture of philanthropy and the ease of talking about money that make them models for other national groups and invaluable volunteer leaders within the international community.

In addition, there is an increasing number of conferences and workshops at which heads of school have a chance to speak openly with one another and to observe that those schools with a professional development program are stronger and better prepared for the future. Thereafter, heads, trustees, and senior administrators are more frequently willing to establish their own development offices. There is an increasing demand for experienced development directors.

Finally, there is true camaraderie among those working in development in international schools, perhaps because of the added moral support needed in the face of shared challenges. These development "pioneers" are creating new standards and best practices in this new environment. No matter what the cultural differences or the language spoken, the generosity of advancement officers toward each other is now the same around the globe.

CHAPTER 4

Creating a Culture of Philanthropy

By Anne Seltzer

Giving is contagious. Philanthropy is infectious. Once it starts, it catches on.

The term "culture of philanthropy" is used often to describe the willingness of all constituents to support their school generously and consistently. Building this culture is one of the development office's most important challenges; the effort provides both short- and long-term rewards.

Discussions with donors about philanthropy should start with a positive message about giving back. Rather than focusing on the percentage who have not given, talk about those who have. Both donors and the larger community will respond better to the message that the school has long enjoyed generous, regular voluntary support from its parents, alumni, grandparents, and parents of alumni.

BENEFITS OF A STRONG CULTURE OF PHILANTHROPY

A strong culture of philanthropy provides many benefits:

- Less time spent educating the constituency about the need for giving and more time spent talking about the mission and needs of the school

- More of development professionals' time spent securing major gifts and less time spent asking for smaller annual gifts

- Less time spent chasing down gifts at the last minute

- More time spent nurturing the major, long-term relationships that lead to transformative gifts

- Greater confidence in talking about the financial needs of the school

- A sense of common responsibility for supporting the school among constituents

Building a strong culture of philanthropy takes time and requires consistent messages. It takes a series of well-planned steps to raise sights and to set goals. However, it is imperative to a school's sustainability that this culture be nurtured carefully.

Here are two questions to consider:

- Does a strong culture of philanthropy exist now? What is the evidence?

- How can this culture be developed or strengthened?

RATE THE SCHOOL'S CULTURE OF PHILANTHROPY

The following checklist provides a helpful tool for educating the board or the staff.

1= weak, needs work   2=okay, average   3=stellar, pleased with efforts and attitude

SCORE

1. The head of school and the board chair actively support the development office.   _____

2. One hundred percent of the board supports the annual, capital, and planned giving programs at a meaningful level. _____

3. New parents are not surprised by the first gift request.   _____

4. Faculty and staff give to the annual fund at or close to 100 percent.   _____

5. There is a high level of participation in all
    development programs.   _____

6. Student philanthropy is encouraged.   _____

7. Donors are well stewarded and thanked often.   _____

8. Alumni come back and give back.   _____

9. Volunteers volunteer to solicit and agree to be trained. _____

10. Campaigns generate excitement and pride.   _____

11. The admissions office talks easily about philanthropy.   _____

12. The development staff is well-known throughout the
    school, and the office and program are viewed favorably. _____

TOTAL   _____

Add up the scores:

33–36 — Strong culture of philanthropy
30–32 = Good culture of philanthropy
25–29 = Average culture of philanthropy
1–25 = Weak culture of philanthropy

TWELVE STEPS TO BUILDING A STRONG CULTURE OF PHILANTHROPY

1. The head of school and the board chair actively support the development office.

All philanthropy starts at the leadership level. It is imperative that the head of school and the board chair are comfortable talking about philanthropy and exemplify the best practices by making their gifts early and at a meaningful level. It is equally important that they support all initiatives of the development office. If trustees are uncomfortable talking about giving to the school, find others who can fulfill this important role and give them a platform.

TIP: Ask the head of school or the board chair to come into the development office frequently to sign letters so that these school leaders meet, know, and are visible to the entire development staff.

2. One hundred percent of the board supports the annual, capital, and planned giving programs at a meaningful level.

The board must support all fund-raising programs in order to set the standard for other donors. Board giving should be in the range of 25 percent of the annual fund goal and 30 percent of a campaign goal. If this expectation is out of line for the present board, it should inform a discussion about future board composition. The expectation of voluntary support should be made clear during the recruitment of new trustees. It is important that the trustee responsible for board recruitment (often the chair of the Committee on Trustees) be comfortable with these discussions. A written trustee job description that reinforces this expectation should be shared with potential trustees during the recruitment process.

Building a strong board of trustees that understands philanthropy may be one of the most important ways to ensure the financial sustainability of a school.

3. New parents are not surprised by the first gift request.

More and more parents at independent schools are new to the development process; they do not understand the role of the annual fund or the need for a capital campaign. Part of a development professional's role is talking to parents who may never have made a philanthropic gift about the importance of making a gift above and beyond the tuitions they may struggle to pay. A careful and consistent process of education is essential and must start early. Many schools start the conversation about giving at the admissions stage (and they display the annual report in the admissions office); other schools introduce it at the opening parent meeting in the fall and follow up with a well-written letter from the head of school explaining the need for voluntary support. All parents should be asked to give to the annual fund during their first year at the school. However, before the first gift request, it is important to educate new parents about the school's dependence on voluntary annual support beyond tuition and about any capital campaigns in progress.

TIP: Before approaching a new family for an annual fund gift, imagine being asked to make a philanthropic gift for the first time. What would help create a sense of comfort for a new donor? What information would help relieve a new donor's anxiety? What would help convince a new donor that making a gift is a positive experience?

4. Faculty and staff give to the annual fund at or close to 100 percent.

Is it important that faculty and staff give at or close to 100 percent to annual fund drives? Those in the corporate world are not asked to give back part of their compensation to support the greater good of the company or firm. However, this is a key difference between the corporate sector, which is profit-based, and the nonprofit sector, which is mission-based. The faculty and staff must believe in the mission and have such pride in the school that they voluntarily give back in order to set the standard of philanthropic giving. In the case of educators whose incomes are consistently below their worth, the emphasis should be on participation rather than the actual amount of a gift. Schools are communities. The more everyone supports the mission and understands the importance of voluntary support, the stronger the bonds of the community will be.

It is important that the solicitor asking the faculty and staff to make a gift has credibility among this group. Often, a respected faculty member is the best person to make the case for support.

A case in point: When The Reynolds School was applying for a matching grant from a local foundation, part of the match depended on the participation of faculty and staff. The head of school and a long-standing faculty member addressed the faculty and asked for their support. They also asked the faculty and staff to learn as much as possible about the grant application for new science labs and to be positive spokespeople for the need in the wider community.

TIP: If the development officers make the first annual fund gifts, they are sending a clear message about their own commitment.

5. There is a high level of participation in all development programs.

High levels of participation in all development efforts help build a strong culture of philanthropy at a school.

There are three reasons to take a broader, more inclusive view of fund raising:

- A mature and schoolwide culture of philanthropy needs broad-based support as well as support at the top.
- Some of the largest gifts come from long-term relationships with donors who may start out making small gifts.

- School loyalty is measured by overall support, not just the support of the wealthiest constituents.

While it may appear more cost-effective to concentrate on the top of the giving pyramid to meet fund-raising goals, schools should not rely only on the top 10 percent of their donor base for support. All donors should be appreciated, listened to, and treated as partners. They should be educated about the different roles of the annual fund, capital campaigns, and special events. Special events often draw a wider base of support. While this is good for school spirit, development officers must be careful not to commit to too many time-consuming special events.

6. Student philanthropy is encouraged.

Education about giving back should start with present students who are philanthropic and idealistic by nature. They are the first to volunteer to raise money for an international catastrophe or a local need. The development office can provide a valuable service by helping students ask wise questions about the charities they choose to support. As students become better informed about their fund raising, they will begin a lifelong habit of giving back. Instead of objecting to the causes students take up because they interfere with the school's fund-raising efforts, it is wiser to encourage students to target and to research their philanthropic interests. A few schools have had great success with student courses on philanthropy.

TIP: Help the senior class plan a graduation gift to the school. Teach those students the basics of good fund raising. Take their efforts seriously.

7. Donors are well stewarded and thanked often.

A good development office consistently stewards its donors. A culture of philanthropy exists in a school at which donors feel adequately thanked and understand that their gifts are being used in the way they had intended. This acknowledgment goes beyond annual reports (a necessary first step in acknowledging donors) and includes ongoing attention and appreciation from the development staff. Avoid the complaint too often heard from a donor: "They spend more time badgering me for the gift I haven't yet given than thanking me for gifts I have given." In a school with a small development office, this extra step of stewardship may appear overwhelming, but it is no less important. A small development staff must be especially creative about ways to thank donors in an ongoing and meaningful way.

TIP: Spend the first week of the summer working on stewardship letters to all donors. Make these letters and/or visits as personal as possible.

8. Alumni come back and give back.

At a school that attracts generous giving, alumni come back and give back. A boarding school has an easier time staying in touch with alumni. An elementary day school has a particular challenge. However, no matter how difficult the challenge, alumni are an important constituency and can provide valuable philanthropic dollars. Two groups provide a natural starting place for alumni giving: (a) past alumni trustees who have been close to and have supported the school and (b) young alumni whose memories of the school are more recent. Establish a goal of nominating one to three young alumni to the board of trustees in the near future. Choose these first young alumni trustees carefully, focusing on their ability to bring back their peers, to work well with an older group of trustees, and to understand the importance of philanthropic giving, no matter what the level.

TIP: Don't lose the allegiance of past trustees. List their names in public places and in annual reports. Continue to treat them as an important part of the school community.

9. Volunteers volunteer to solicit and agree to be trained.

All development work depends on good volunteers. Peer solicitations are often the most successful. Stress the importance of solicitor training; make it fun and interactive. Consider bringing in an outside person to do the training. Take on the reluctant volunteer who says, "I will do anything except ask for money" as a particular challenge. Make sure that all volunteer solicitors are given accurate information and are fully supported by the development office. The more clarity given to the process of solicitation and the more experience a group of volunteers has, the more effective their efforts will be.

TIP: Pair a reluctant volunteer solicitor with an experienced one, and make sure the first gift request is likely to be successful.

10. Campaigns generate excitement and pride.

A culture of philanthropy is all about institutional pride, and a successful, well-executed campaign builds this pride. It dramatically increases the buzz about giving; it raises the sights of the donor pool. Good campaigns train committed volunteers who help for years to come. They provide opportunities for donors to give generously to a cause that they believe in and to share that belief publicly and widely. Because campaigns are so important to the financial and emotional health of a school, it is critical that all campaigns be impeccably planned well before they begin.

11. The admissions office talks easily about philanthropy.

Building a strong financial base for a school is not solely the responsibility of the development office. All school administrators should have a basic understanding of the finances of the school and of its fund-raising goals. This is especially true of the admissions office where families are first introduced to the school. The admissions office should work in concert with the development office to educate parents about philanthropic expectations.

> **TIP:** Schools whose admissions offices are named in honor of or in memory of a school family are showcasing philanthropy to potential parents.

12. The development staff is well-known throughout the school, and the office and program are viewed favorably.

It is wise to locate development offices in the heart of the campus and to provide space for parents and alumni to work and to socialize. It is helpful if development officers sit with faculty and students at lunch. It is important for the head of school to be as proud of his or her development officers as he or she is of the faculty. It is essential that the development director remind the faculty that money raised is a reflection of the good work the teachers do every day.

Philanthropy must be seen as a positive value throughout a school. A culture of philanthropy is built by careful planning, consistent messages, and ongoing education.

Remember, all of these steps take time and honest talk about giving. As schools think actively about building a culture of philanthropy, stress the fact that schools are philanthropic communities. Emphasize the positive. Brag about the success of the annual fund and about exciting gifts that reflect a donor's loyalty and gratitude.

Great stories of philanthropy abound at independent schools. Tell them with pride.

THE
PROGRAMS

CHAPTER 5

The Annual Fund: A Donor's First Gift

By Leslie Hutchens

O n the philanthropy pyramid, the annual fund is the foundation. The stronger the foundation, the stronger the pyramid will be. It is through the annual fund that close relationships are formed with future major donors and with the next generation of volunteers. The capital campaign chair of tomorrow and the major donors of the next decade are working on the annual fund today.

The annual fund provides operating funds for the current year. This vital income helps bridge the gap between tuition revenue and the true cost of an education. Most annual fund gifts are unrestricted. However, some schools permit donors to give designated annual gifts that help meet a specific budgeted need. Both unrestricted and designated annual gifts must be spent in the fiscal year in which they are received.

Donors sometimes confuse annual fund gifts with capital or endowment gifts. There are three key differences:

1. Annual fund gifts support the operating budget of the current year. Capital gifts underwrite new facilities or building renovations. Endowment gifts are invested in perpetuity, and only a portion of the interest income is spent each year, often for a particular purpose.

2. Annual fund pledges must be paid in full by the end of each fiscal

year while capital or endowment campaigns almost always permit multi-year pledges.

3. The annual fund ends with each fiscal year. The day after one fiscal year ends, both a new annual fund campaign and a new fiscal year begin. Capital and endowment campaigns typically take place over several years.

GOAL SETTING

Annual fund planning begins with effective goal setting. To understand how much can be raised (as opposed to how much the school wishes could be raised) the planners review the results of the previous year. They pay particular attention to the following:

- LYBUNTs (donors who made annual fund gifts "Last Year But Unfortunately Not This") and SYBUNTs (donors who made annual fund gifts "Some Years But Unfortunately Not This"). These constituents already have an understanding of the importance of the annual fund and have demonstrated their willingness to give.

- Top prospects (those who are in the top 10 percent of the donor pool in terms of potential to give). Typically, 80 to 90 percent of annual fund dollars come from 10 to 20 percent of a school's donors.

- Groups that will have a special reason to give during the upcoming year. These include alumni celebrating a reunion, parents of graduating seniors, and parents new to the community.

Once the potential has been analyzed, a feasible goal can be set. To build success into the process, the goal should be less than the amount that could potentially be raised due to the fact that, unfortunately, not all donors will give the amount requested. However, a truly successful annual fund will grow at a rate faster than the budget grows. Experienced fund raisers know that they should project steady annual increases rather than a giant gain in any one year.

THE CALENDAR

A well-run annual fund should have a 12-month calendar beginning in July of one year and ending in June of the next.

Summer is the time to plan the campaign. The development staff looks back on the previous annual fund drive and identifies those strategies and initiatives that were most successful and those that were least successful. They evaluate the program by talking to development peers, volunteers, and selected donors. Each year, they design new approaches.

Summer is also the time to begin drafting solicitation letters and to order letterhead, pledge cards, phonathon cards, and other materials.

When the school year starts, annual fund solicitations begin. All potential donors should be contacted at least once, if not twice, before the end of December by mail, phone, or in person. Many prospects, especially those who give more than $1,000, contribute each year at a particular time. The staff should pay attention to those giving patterns.

December is a high-volume month for gifts as many donors will respond before the end of the tax year. Therefore, it is wise to send a December reminder.

Winter and early spring are the best times to pause and look closely at progress to date. Review special constituency segments, such as new parents or alumni reunion classes. Approach habitual donors who have not yet given.

The final annual fund push comes during the spring. Re-contact potential donors who have not yet made a gift. Much like December, June is a busy month for last-minute donors.

In addition to breaking the year into quarters, the annual fund timeline should include a schedule for each constituency group. From a marketing perspective, the timing of solicitations is important. The most effective appeals coincide with a meaningful moment. For example, the first fall solicitation might refer to the excitement of a new school year.

THE SOLICITATION

The annual fund reaches out to potential donors in several ways.

1. Direct Mail

A letter or a brochure (or a letter with a brochure) sent to all constituents is the backbone of the annual fund. When used effectively, direct mail provides an opportunity to state the case for support in detail as follows:

- Selling the special strengths and uniqueness of the school

- Documenting the need

- Creating a sense of urgency

- Explaining how and when gifts should be made

- Conveying gratitude for support

A brochure and a letter from a respected member of the community highlighting a tradition or bringing back fond memories create a compelling direct mail package.

However, even the best direct mail piece is a one-sided conversation. The school presents the case for support, but the recipient cannot ask questions.

2. Phonathons

Calling a prospective donor to seek his or her support is an effective follow-up to direct mail. A traditional phonathon brings volunteers together at a specific place and time to make calls. Carefully pair callers and prospects. For example, an alumnus might call classmates; a senior parent might call peers.

The advantage of a phonathon is that it allows a two-way conversation about the importance of the annual fund. If the prospect has questions, the volunteer can address them immediately. The disadvantage of a phonathon is that it is a challenge to find a good time to call. Typically, phonathons are held after work, from 6 p.m. to 9 p.m., for example, a busy time for parents who might not answer the phone. In addition, many households now have caller I.D. and can monitor calls. This problem can be avoided by asking volunteers to use personal cell phones or to make calls from their offices or homes.

The value that personal contact adds to annual fund solicitations cannot be overestimated. However, there is a clear trend toward the new informal phonathon format in which volunteers call off-site on their own schedules and from their own phones.

3. The Visit

A personal visit is both the most effective and the most time-consuming method of solicitation. Sitting down with a prospect to talk about the annual fund helps the prospect feel invested in the institution and understand the impact of a gift. The prospect can ask questions, and the solicitor can read nonverbal communication signals and adjust the conversation accordingly. For example, if the prospect responds to the case for the financial aid program, the solicitor can emphasize the impact of annual fund gifts on financial aid students. Donors can better understand that their gifts make a difference. However, not all prospects can be seen in person. Reserve personal visits for those prospects with the highest gift potential.

4. E-mail

During recent years, development professionals have been using e-mail with increasing frequency to seek annual fund gifts. E-mail does not have the flow of a conversation, but there is an opportunity to answer a question if the prospect responds. In addition, like direct mail, e-mail permits individual solicitors to make a case for support. Finally, recipients may open e-mail messages when it is convenient, while phone calls are made at a set time and must be repeated if the prospect is not reached.

These methods are not the only forms of annual fund solicitations. Using modern technology, annual fund professionals are finding new ways to reach out to the community. In the years to come, many additional solicitation techniques will emerge. (See Chapter 15.)

SEGMENTATION AND PERSONALIZATION

Through the segmentation of appeals, address the specific interests and circumstances of different constituent groups. Because each group has a different relationship with the school, each may have a different reason for supporting it. Parents, for example, may consider their annual gifts an investment in the school today, while alumni are likely to view annual gifts as an expression of appreciation for experiences they had in the past.

The first step is to segment large constituencies such as alumni, parents, grandparents, and parents of alumni. From there, narrow each group further.

Design different approaches for young alumni, reunion classes, alumni by decade, or alumni by class year. Segment parents into smaller segments also, such as new parents, parents who are also alumni, parents of seniors, or parents of students in a particular grade.

A segmented appeal is only part of the challenge; personalization is the other part. To make prospects feel important, write the appeal just for them. Replace "Dear Friend" with "Dear Jane." Add a reunion year or a grandchild's name. Personalization takes more time. However, it is always worth the effort.

VOLUNTEERS

Finding and recruiting good volunteers to solicit gifts is a key challenge. The best annual fund volunteers are generous and consistent donors who lead by example. They are often able to recommend and recruit new members of the annual fund volunteer team.

Volunteers make a significant contribution by soliciting peers when they are properly matched to prospects. For alumni, a class agent system of volunteers works well. Competition between class agents can help reach more ambitious dollar and participation goals.

Parents can often have the greatest success when contacting other parents in their children's classes. At day schools, parents have the advantage of proximity and are able to schedule more personal visits.

DATA AND REPORTS

Since there is a short time to reach the goal, constant monitoring of progress is essential. Just as a pilot needs to check flight instruments and make necessary course corrections, so an annual fund director must monitor progress constantly throughout the year. Pay particular attention to total cash and pledges; total cash received; and the total number of donors, new donors, and LYBUNTs. Meet at least half of the annual fund goal, if not more, halfway through the fiscal year.

If the data reports reveal that appropriate progress is not being made, a course correction is in order. Should a particular segment be solicited again?

Should more attention be given to LYBUNTs? Are gift levels increasing or decreasing? The successful annual fund director uses regular database reports to stay ahead of the goal.

STEWARDSHIP

Through stewardship after the gift, donors understand that their support is deeply appreciated and that the annual fund has a meaningful impact on the welfare of the school and its students. Furthermore, well-stewarded donors are likely to give again.

Take the time to tell donors how important they are. Donors expect the standard IRS gift acknowledgment, but also include a warm thank-you letter. If a form letter is used, add a personal handwritten note whenever possible. Let the donors know that you notice and appreciate their support.

Class agents and other solicitors should also write thank-you notes to donors from whom they have sought support. The faculty might do a thank-a-thon. Letters or calls from the head of school are always meaningful.

Gift clubs are another way of thanking donors. Because IRS regulations dictate that the value of the benefits of gift club membership cannot exceed a certain percentage of the gift, the clubs should be used for recognition only (as in the annual report) and should not offer other costly advantages.

Gift clubs can also create the incentive for increased gifts. The highest gift club should be at a lofty (and sustainable) level but, at the same time, low enough to have at least one or two members each year. At some schools, this will be a $10,000 gift club, while others may have a core of leadership donors who can sustain their giving at $25,000 and who should be singled out for recognition in a top gift club.

Often, the head of school hosts a reception for donors of $1,000 or more. This is yet another way to make the donors feel that their gifts are appreciated and that they have had a positive impact on the school.

TEAMWORK

The annual fund does not exist in a vacuum. To the contrary, fund-raising programs achieve their potential only if there is cooperation within the development office.

Major gift officers rely on annual fund professionals to identify new prospects and to begin to cultivate them. The first gift a major prospect makes is most often to the annual fund. Similarly, annual fund professionals rely on major gift officers and capital campaign directors to make sure that the importance of continuing annual support is stressed during solicitations for larger gifts. When a school's fund raisers work together, everyone benefits.

The annual fund staff and the alumni relations office must also work together. The "friend raising" done by the alumni staff very often translates into increased participation in fund raising. Coordinate the alumni and annual giving mailings and calendars in order to present a well-timed and consistent message.

Close collaboration with communications and publications personnel is essential. Publication professionals can help design and write brochures, proofread letters, and navigate the mail system. Coordinate mailings, such as the annual report and newsletters, with annual fund appeals.

THE FAMILY OF FUNDS

An annual giving approach that has become popular is the family of funds. Schools are using this marketing tool to let donors choose to allocate their gifts to one or more broad gift opportunities, such as the arts, athletics, financial aid, faculty, campus maintenance, or technology. The funds contributed provide operating budget relief only, not additional restricted funds for a particular area of school life. An accompanying disclaimer explains that the board of trustees retains the discretion to use these annual giving proceeds to support the school's general operations should contributions for a particular purpose exceed the expenditure limits provided in that year's operating budget.

The family-of-funds approach is a marketing device only; it does not change the board-designated allocation of funds. However, many annual fund directors have found that offering donors the opportunity to direct their gifts fosters more generous support and helps the school provide a consistent message each year.

Finally, working closely with the staff member who manages the database is vital. The annual fund director must understand the process used for entering gifts into the database, be able to read records in the database, and know how to run evaluative reports.

CONCLUSION

The annual fund provides vital operating revenue each year. It must be successfully integrated into the overall fund-raising efforts of the school, and its importance must not be overlooked during capital and endowment campaigns.

Annual fund professionals should be detail-oriented team players and creative thinkers. They should communicate well with both volunteers and donors. And they should be energized by the challenge of a campaign conducted both over a short time period and every year.

CHAPTER 6

Major Gifts: The Essential Element of Fund-Raising Success

By Helen A. Colson

irst and foremost, development is about people, about building and nurturing relationships with those people whose generosity can empower a school. The best fund-raising programs focus on developing top donors. The most effective fund raisers focus on involving top prospects, on giving them a sense of belonging, on seeking their lifetime loyalty and support.

At every independent school, large or small, urban or rural, old or new, fund-raising success depends on major gifts. Therefore, major donor research, cultivation, solicitation, and stewardship are the most important professional challenges for directors of development at all schools and at all times. This chapter focuses on research, cultivation, and stewardship.

No matter how excellent a school, how worthy its plans, or how pressing its needs, it will not receive major gifts unless its major prospects are informed and involved and feel needed and committed. *Major gifts reflect the depth of the donors' commitment rather than the magnitude of the institution's need.*

That's why, no matter what the size of the office and no matter what the size of the campaign, the best major gift fund raisers focus on deepening the best prospects' commitment to the school. These fund raisers understand that every major gift prospect is unique. They cherish their knowledge of the passions and idiosyncrasies that distinguish one major gift prospect from another.

EVERYONE PLAYS A ROLE

The director of development is the orchestra leader of a major gifts program. Even in a one-person shop, the director should devote at least 20 percent of his or her time to major gifts, if the school is to fulfill its fund-raising potential.

Furthermore, in the 21st century, every development staff member is, by definition, a major gifts officer no matter what other assignments or titles he or she may have. Every member of the professional staff should have a portfolio of major gift prospects, and everyone in the office, from the receptionist to the data entry assistant, should know who the school's top prospects are as well as how best to approach and respond to them. Major prospects should be regularly reviewed at development staff meetings; each prospect should have an individual cultivation plan.

However, even though a major gifts program is staff driven, no development director or major gifts officer can build a close relationship with a donor without help. The process usually includes key trustees and volunteers. These people are sometimes referred to as "natural partners" because they have access to the prospective donor and because they are in the best position to determine what kind of approach will be most effective.

The head of school also plays a key role. He or she should be able to recognize the top 10 donors on the soccer field or at a school event and should be able to refer specifically to the ongoing impact of their gifts.

In addition, the faculty (especially long-tenured, beloved teachers) and senior administrators should be educated about the importance of major gifts. Because they have the opportunity to interact with major gift prospects and donors, they, too, have a role to play in cultivating and stewarding major gifts.

Finally, carefully selected volunteers are essential participants in a major gifts program. They serve on major gifts and cultivation committees. They host cultivation events. They help evaluate prospective donors. Without committed volunteers, a major gifts program cannot succeed.

WHO ARE MAJOR GIFT PROSPECTS?

The major gift prospect is an individual whose capacity to give puts him or her in the top 10 percent of the prospect pool. At some schools, this person may have the potential to contribute $10 million; at other schools, a major gift is in the $10,000 range. This essential 10 percent is likely to give 90 percent of the school's total voluntary support. In fact, at many schools, the top 5 percent gives 95 percent.

The typical major gift prospect …

- is affluent.
- is philanthropic.
- has a long-term relationship with the school.
- gives from the heart to support the school's mission.
- takes time to make a decision.
- employs several gift vehicles, often including outright and deferred support.
- seeks professional advice.

He or she may be a young, successful entrepreneur or a wealthy retiree. Most often, he or she is a previous donor who is willing and able to upgrade past support.

Typically, schools need at least three prospects for each major gift it will receive. This is more challenging because, as noted in Chapter 1, there are fewer major gift prospects on the 21st century philanthropic landscape.

However, these fewer donors are making larger gifts. Not long ago, most independent school capital campaigns aimed for one or two $1 million gifts. In today's campaigns, the top gift may be $5 million, $10 million, or, in the case of a few fortunate schools, even more. And there can be as many as five to 15 $1 million pledges.

Within almost all major prospect groups are a few donors — perhaps only one or two — with the ability to make single gifts that can transform a school. These "ultimate gifts" are usually the largest contributions a donor has ever made and the largest gifts a school has ever received. They are perhaps 1,000 to 10,000 times larger than gifts the donor makes on a regular basis. They come from donors with a track record of growing support and a deep commitment that has been nurtured over a long period of time.

THE MAJOR GIFTS PROGRAM PLAN

A professional major gifts program begins with a written plan that establishes the process and timetable for (a) identifying and qualifying major prospects and (b) their cultivation, solicitation, and stewardship. The plan also establishes clear performance expectations for the staff.

Designing the timetable for a major gifts program is an ongoing process. It requires regular focus, but it can't be rushed. Often, the more patient the major gifts officer is, the larger the eventual gift will be.

A successful major gifts program has these characteristics:

- It is permanent and ongoing.
- It is personal and customized.
- It is carefully managed and tracked.
- It is donor focused.
- It is unhurried.
- It is built over time.
- It is inclusive of planned gift options.

The tracking should involve bimonthly goals for and a review of the following:

- The number of new prospects identified
- The number of prospect research files completed
- The number of rating and screening sessions
- The number of cultivation moves
- The number of personal visits

Because major gifts can take many forms, including cash, appreciated securities, real estate, gifts in trust, life insurance, and other outright and deferred contributions, the successful major gifts program must include the marketing of planned gifts. (See Chapter 8.)

ARE MAJOR GIFTS A PRIORITY?

In a school with a professional major gifts program, the development director can answer "yes" to each of the following questions:

1. Is the development staff well trained in major gift philanthropy?
2. Are many of the board members capable of and willing to make major gifts?
3. Does the head of school devote at least 20 percent of his or her time to major donor cultivation, solicitation, and stewardship?
4. Does the development office staff spend time out of the office meeting with major prospects and, at times, with their financial advisors?
5. Is there a joint staff and volunteer major gifts committee that meets regularly, whether or not a capital campaign is in progress?
6. Is there a regularly reviewed list of well-researched major prospects?
7. Is there a clear "moves management" system that tracks each prospect's movement toward a major gift?
8. Is there a major donor stewardship program?
9. Does the school market planned gift options?
10. Has the school invested adequate resources in major gift philanthropy?

RESEARCH AND RATING

A major gifts program begins with donor research. Its purpose is to identify and to evaluate the top 10 percent of the school's prospect pool in terms of capacity to give. Major donor research should be ongoing at all schools, whether or not a capital campaign is in progress or about to begin.

Once staff members have identified a major gift prospect, they should undertake further study — using both outside sources and volunteers within the school — to answer three questions:

1. What is this prospect's financial capacity?

2. How strong is the prospect's current interest in the school?

3. How philanthropic is the prospect?

In order to design an effective cultivation plan, it is not sufficient to calculate major gift potential alone. The donor evaluation process must also focus on readiness to give: the likelihood that the donor will want to make a major gift. The readiness to give level can cover a wide range — from those who are responsive when they are simply told about a need to those who may not respond even after much personal attention.

For many decades, donor research consisted of studying reference books, such as *Who's Who*, *Standard & Poor's*, and *Martindale-Hubbell*. Today, those books and countless other useful databases are online. Computer screening, using a variety of sources in the public domain, can identify potential donors far more accurately and quickly than in the past. Some schools do this research in house; others engage a prospect research firm.

Carefully selected volunteers also play an important role in donor research. Their challenge is to rate and screen potential donors whom they know or know about. At donor evaluation sessions, these volunteers assess gift capacity, identify special interests, suggest appropriate gift vehicles, and predict readiness to give. (For sample prospect rating and screening guidelines, see page 68.)

Those who rate and screen should understand two principles:

1. Rating and screening is a confidential process. Its purpose is to gather facts and insights to make solicitors more sensitive to a prospect's status, feelings, and needs, as well as more successful in obtaining generous support.

2. In rating and screening, it is the quality, rather than the quantity, of information that counts. Providing significant insights about only one prospect on a list of 500 may open the door to a major gift.

Sometimes development officers overlook one important information source: the prospects themselves. Personal contact — whether at social events, homecoming, reunions, fund-raising planning sessions, or basketball games — always provides an opportunity to learn more about an individual's philanthropic interests and special concerns.

The development staff should document and save information and advice gleaned during the research process (along with copies of relevant correspondence, clippings, and memos) in confidential electronic and hard-copy files. The material in those files will help the staff prepare appropriate individual cultivation and stewardship plans and effective solicitation strategies, both now and in the years to come.

CULTIVATION: NOTHING MATTERS MORE

Major donor cultivation follows research but precedes the gift request. It lays the groundwork for both present and future fund-raising success. Cultivation is the process of turning a prospect from an outsider to an insider. What's the difference?

- An outsider is interested in the school; an insider is passionate about its welfare.

- An outsider is aware of an institutional need; an insider is committed to meeting it.

- An outsider is informed about a campaign; an insider feels responsible for its success.

Careful, sensitive major donor cultivation is an important prerequisite to solicitation success. Without effective cultivation, the prospect will know less, care less, and give less. With effective cultivation, the prospect will understand a school's mission and vision, its short- and long-term needs, and the impact that major gift philanthropy can have.

A good cultivation process builds a close relationship, bonding the donor to the school. Successful cultivators put themselves in the donor's position. They focus less on the institution's goals and timetables and more on the donor's objectives and needs. They look for the best match between the two.

Prospects should not be solicited until they have been individually educated, interested, and motivated. Don't celebrate if a major gift prospect gives $250,000 before cultivation. After a proper courtship, he or she might have given much more.

Schools should cultivate their major prospects irrespective of the economy's ups and downs. For the very high net-worth donor, a major drop in the market often does not affect giving decisions, although he or she may wish to give one year at a time rather than make a multiyear pledge. It is important to remember that the vast majority of major prospects are making gifts below their true potential.

The best major donor cultivation is candid, one-on-one, and face-to-face. Here is what the cultivator's words and deeds should suggest to the prospect: "Many people regard you as a potential leader at this school. We feel that if you become knowledgeable and enthusiastic about our goals, we can benefit significantly from your interest, judgment, and support. We'd like to bring you into the inner circle of our school."

The cultivator aims to accomplish the following:

- Seek the prospect's friendship and respect

- Demonstrate to the prospect why he or she should believe in and become personally invested in the school's welfare

- Persuade the prospect that a project or campaign will have a significant impact and is worthy of particularly generous support

- Help the prospect understand how important major gifts are to a campaign's success and how personally rewarding major gift philanthropy can be

Cultivation consists of a series of contacts designed to bring a potential donor closer to the school:

- Lunch or dinner at which a trustee or other volunteer shares information or seeks advice

- Morning coffee with the head of school to learn more about the school's 21st century goals and priorities

- A personal tour of a new facility under construction

- The sharing of a draft strategic plan or case statement with a request for advice

- An invitation to share expertise, as appropriate, with a class or student club

- An invitation to attend a board of trustees or development staff meeting to explain why he or she is a generous investor in the school

- The opportunity to serve on a school committee or to help with a school event

- A request to hold a cultivation event at the prospect's home

These contacts should be regular, frequent, individual, face-to-face, well planned, and carefully documented. They should be coordinated with other friend-making and fund-raising programs and should be frequently reviewed and evaluated. They should take into account the nature of the prospect's current relationship with the school and his or her particular interests or experiences.

These contacts are referred to as "moves," a concept developed in the 1970s by G.T. (Buck) Smith during his tenure at Cornell University and refined by his Cornell colleague, David Dunlop. According to Smith, moves are intended to develop the prospect's awareness of, knowledge of, interest in, involvement with, and eventual commitment to an institution and its mission. The purpose of the moves is to keep the school in the hearts and minds of prospects and previous donors on a regular basis.

Many schools are conscientious about scheduling contacts with each of their top prospects each month. They nurture relationships with their major prospects at private dinners, during reunion weekends, and at special events. They further strengthen the ties though personal notes and spontaneous telephone calls.

During an effective cultivation process, the major gift prospect goes through six stages in relating to an institutional need:

1. Awareness

2. Knowledge

3. Interest

4. Caring

5. Participation

6. Commitment

From the school's point of view, courting the major gift prospect involves five steps:

1. Identify
2. Inform
3. Interest
4. Involve
5. Invest

When the donor is committed to the school and personally invested in its welfare, he or she is ready to make a generous major gift.

STEWARDSHIP

Stewardship is cultivation after the gift. It is the process of maintaining and nurturing a donor's continuing relationship to the school, of making him or her feel good about the gift. It provides an opportunity to deepen a donor's relationship to the school. When it is well done, it leads to continued and increasing levels of support.

Basic to good gift stewardship are (1) prompt and warm thanks and (2) the assurance — repeated over and over again — that the gift is having a significant impact on the school and is being used as the donor requested. Above all, gift acknowledgment should be accurate. A misspelled or inaccurate name can leave a lasting negative impression.

Acknowledgment of a very large gift should also reflect its significance to the school. A telephone call from the school head or a hand-delivered letter from the campaign chair should come on the day on which the gift is received. Thereafter, others should send personal and meaningful expressions of sincere gratitude.

Furthermore, leadership gift acknowledgment should never end. The donor who provides the naming gift for an arts center should be invited not only to the dedication but also to plays and musicals in future years. The donor whose gift was used to name the gym should be an honored guest at major sports events many years hence.

Stewardship should be as individually geared as cultivation is. It should reflect an understanding of the donor's priorities, interests, motivations, and history with the school. Many schools send a special letter to major donors each year on the anniversary of their gifts. Individual reports should be sent annually to major donors of both restricted and unrestricted gifts. These reports should explain how the money has been spent and reiterate the school's gratitude. It may be more challenging to write to the donor of an unrestricted gift. However, bear in mind that such donors are often those who are the most loyal, who care the most, and who have the most confidence in the school.

Schools should steward major donors even when their giving levels drop during economically challenging times. A donor who has considered the school worthy of a major gift in the past may give generously once again when his or her personal circumstances improve. And the donor who has given generously in the past deserves ongoing thanks, irrespective of his or her personal circumstances.

What if the school has not been a good steward? How should staff or volunteers approach a benefactor long ignored? Most experienced fund raisers agree that it's never too late for stewardship to begin. A dinner to honor a leadership donor a decade after his or her gift can be a first step to reconnecting a major prospect with the school.

In an increasingly competitive philanthropic environment, stewardship has never been more important. Compared to colleges and universities, the number of major gift prospects at most independent schools is small. Therefore, each top prospect is a treasure who should be treated with sensitivity and care before, during, and after the gift request. Major gift prospects — that essential 10 percent — should know that they are important and needed — because they are!

MAJOR PROSPECT
Rating and Screening Guidelines

Rating

A. Please use the following numerical rating codes to refer to a prospect's potential for *total giving to all charities over a three-year period:*

1. $1,000,000 and above
2. $500,000–$1,000,000
3. $100,000–$500,000
4. $25,000–$100,000

B. Please give every prospect you rate a letter code based on his or her *current readiness* to give to the school the largest gift of which he or she is capable:

a. Ready to give
b. Needs some cultivation
c. Needs a great deal of additional cultivation
d. Unlikely to give to this campaign

C. Please add a "star" if it is appropriate to ask the prospect to leave a bequest to the school in his or her will. Please add a "check" if he or she is likely to be interested in another type of planned gift.

Screening

A. Review your list quickly.

B. Evaluate only those you know personally. Skip those you do not know. Do not be concerned if you know only a few prospects on the list.

C. Base your fiscal estimate on what you believe a prospect *can* give to *all charities over a three-year period*, if sufficiently interested, and not on what you think he or she will give to your school.

D. Consider your opinion to be an *estimate* of potential. We are not depending on you alone for definitive data. Your evaluation will be considered in light of many other opinions and facts.

Additional Information

A. In the course of rating, indicate the names of prospects for whom you might be an appropriate solicitor. Indicate as well your suggestions of appropriate solicitors for others.

B. In addition, when possible, note the following:

1. Components of the campaign that are most likely to interest the prospect
2. Other family members who might join the prospect in making a group gift
3. The prospect's potential interest in a named gift
4. The prospect's other charitable interests

CHAPTER 7

Capital Campaigns: Practices and Principles

By Tracy G. Savage, Andrew Hamlin, and Kathy Schulte

In the life of virtually every independent school, there are times when the need for extra, significant gift support is clear and urgent, and school leaders announce, "We need a campaign!"

Such a time might be when the goals of a carefully developed strategic plan require additional money or when a critical need for funding appears suddenly. In some instances, it's the physical facilities "arms race" — when competition for applicants drives peer schools to outdo each other's campus buildings — that creates the demand for new funds. Increasingly, many schools use disciplined, long-range financial projections in their budget planning that often reveal a need for larger, more stable "reserves"; hence, the growing number of schools who seek endowment gifts to bolster their financial sustainability.

Whatever the impetus for launching a major campaign, there are some common principles and a few best practices that have traditionally characterized the most successful of these fund-raising endeavors. Some of these campaign principles and practices are based in science — quantitative, measurable, data-driven modeling with proven results. Other campaign practices are more the province of art — blending subjective, emotional, anecdotal human ideas, intuition, and fund-raising experience. The most salient of both kinds of principles and practices — scientific and artistic — make up the meat of this chapter.

Common to all campaigns are the several key elements and considerations listed below.

- Sequence, calendar, and key decision points

- The case statement

- Leadership and volunteers

- Campaign staffing and budget

- Prospects

At the same time, every school is distinct, so that boilerplate formulae are inadequate. Most generous donors are motivated by the special character and mission of a school and by the proposed use of the funds far more than by the nature or conduct of the campaign itself. Hence, it is important to design a campaign that really "fits" the school — in style, structure, and execution.

In the end, a campaign is a dynamic organism. It evolves, transforms itself, reinvents itself, slows with fatigue, and leaps forward with enormous bursts of energy, and almost never unfolds the way it was planned. Even so, perhaps the single most common trait of a successful campaign is the depth and quality of planning that precedes its launch. And although a major campaign sometimes seems to have a life of its own, we know for sure that the bones and the muscles and the heart of this complex organism are always, only, and ever the people who are making the campaign happen.

SEQUENCE, CALENDAR, AND KEY DECISION POINTS

If a major campaign is an engine that drives the activity of fund raising, then, like the locomotive, there is an order, an arrangement, of tasks that truly matter if the campaign engine is to run smoothly. Put simply, an experienced engineer knows how far ahead the railroad tracks must be clear before pulling out of the station. This example is elementary but no more so than, say, asking a lead prospect for a gift before knowing how the funds will be used or deciding how long the campaign will last before setting the dollar goal and analyzing the pool of potential donors.

Sequence Makes a Difference

Campaigns are fraught with the unknown. How much can the school raise? How long will it take? Will the new building inspire a big gift? Will adding a major gifts officer increase the pledge totals? Will a change in school leadership be good or bad? Will volunteers make it harder or easier? Should the campaign go public sooner?

These questions can be positively daunting in the beginning. However, with each campaign step — in the right order — new information comes to light about donors, leadership, the case, the goal, etc. Therefore, the sequence of activity throughout the campaign is vital. Without a good sequence, good decision-making along the way is almost impossible. Chart A (see the following pages) suggests a simple sequence for the basic components of a comprehensive school campaign.

Not every school will utilize every step in Chart A, and certainly the timeframe of the steps may be different for different schools. These steps are neither inviolate nor inflexible, but they do represent a logical order in which to tackle key campaign activities. Let's highlight a few of these steps and think a bit about why the order matters.

Setting a Working Dollar Goal

All too often, school leaders and trustees develop a gut feeling about an achievable goal. Despite the occasional accuracy of such feelings, the more reliable sequence would be (a) agree on strategic imperatives; (b) cost them out carefully, not only for a building project but for an endowment drive (for which the school must be able to explain how, exactly, X dollars will have the desired impact, given the endowment spending policy); (c) analyze the wealth capacity of the donor pool; (d) test the inclination of the donor pool to support the school's funding needs; and then (e) set a working dollar goal.

Even after a campaign has begun, many schools retain the concept and flexibility of a working goal until the nucleus fund goal (leadership gifts goal before the public phase is launched) is achieved. Only when the public phase gets underway do they set a final dollar goal.

CHART A: CAPITAL CAMPAIGN PLANNING CALENDAR

	Year One														
	J	F	M	A	M	J	J	A	S	O	N	D			
Strategic Planning Completed	▓														
Wealth Screening Conducted	▓		▓												
Program Assessment/Staffing Review		▓		▓											
Prospect Qualification/Cultivation	▓	▓	▓	▓	▓	▓	▓	▓	▓	▓	▓	▓			
CC Early Phase Communication Strategy				▓	▓			▓							
Program & Staffing Adjustments						▓	▓								
CC Advisory Group Identified/Recruited							▓	▓			▓				
Facilities Needs Explored/Costed							▓	▓	▓	▓	▓				
Endowment Needs Explored/Costed							▓	▓	▓	▓	▓				
CC Prospectus Developed											▓	▓			
Gift Acceptance Policies Developed															
Feasibility Study/Testing															
Feasibility Report & Recommendations															
Campaign Leadership/Volunteer Recruited															
CC Case Revised/Refined															
CC Calendar Developed															
CC Budget Developed															
Final CC Communications Plan Developed															
CC Goal/Scope/Purposes Adopted															
Trustee/Leadership Solicitations															

	Year Two													Year Three											
	J	F	M	A	M	J	J	A	S	O	N	D		J	F	M	A	M	J	J	A	S	O	N	D

Appointing Campaign Leaders

This step is often taken either too early or too late. Occasionally, a school or board member will leap forward to invite an individual to chair an upcoming campaign before careful consultation with development professionals and trustees. If this individual is not an ideal choice, the campaign may be saddled with poor leadership from the beginning, a difficulty that can truly undermine the campaign's success.

On the other hand, some schools wait too long to appoint campaign leaders. It is essential that those individuals who emerge as the greatest fundraising champions are brought along early on so that they become personally invested in the elements of the case, in the analysis of the top donors, in the campaign goal, and in the success of the campaign itself. That depth of engagement is critical to the grooming of great campaign leaders and hard to generate in an individual who boards the train long after it has left the station.

Creating and Producing Campaign Materials and Marketing Aids

The creation of visual aids — the case statement, the campaign CD, the video or DVD, all the promotional tools used to market the campaign — often absorbs the energy and attention of trustees and school leaders much too early in campaign planning. Because these materials can be expensive and, in some cases, will be widely distributed, their production is often better delayed for the public phase. What if the nucleus goal changes or a new building initiative emerges or the campaign timeline is altered? It takes very little time for fancy materials to become stale and out-of-date. Furthermore, some of the most generous giving occurs early, when donors feel that they can set a pace, when they can help determine the style of the campaign. Expansive, polished campaign materials often convey the impression that there's no opportunity for that kind of major donor input.

Conducting a Feasibility Study or Other Capacity/Feasibility Testing

One of the most common missteps in preparing for a campaign is launching a feasibility study too soon. The best kind of feasibility testing is different for every school; there are alternative, expanded, refined, hybridized, adaptive models for testing a campaign's likelihood of success. Exploring and deciding which feasibility model works best takes time.

In addition, feasibility testing requires that the school's priorities and funding needs have been carefully determined and endorsed by the board and that they have been articulated well enough to share with potential donors who will participate in the testing. This process can take months.

Finally, if the model used is the traditional feasibility study based on individual interviews, its execution is but a snapshot in time — and the results are, therefore, only valid for a relatively short period. Hence, the most helpful feasibility testing occurs late in campaign planning and should be one of the last steps taken before the board agrees to move ahead with the campaign and begin solicitation.

Calendar

As campaign goals have become larger, campaign calendars have become longer. In the independent school world, it is not uncommon to see a campaign with a five-year active solicitation period and a three- to five-year pledge collection period immediately following. In fact, many schools plan their next campaign while still collecting pledge payments from the last.

There is no magic number of months or years for a campaign's duration. There are, however, several kinds of fatigue that bear monitoring in the lengthy campaign. First, the broader population of donors should feel the freshness of the campaign messages and aspirations. Since campaign marketing is quieter and often limited to top prospects during the nucleus phase, it is the length of the public phase that bears watching.

The second area of possible fatigue is that of the campaign's leadership. Many outstanding volunteers may step up to champion a big campaign; few of them can make a campaign their highest priority for eight or 10 years. Some schools shift campaign leadership to a second team during the public phase; others ask co-chairs to share the leadership. It is important, however, not to allow great campaign leaders to finish their service exhausted and depleted.

Key Decision Points

A few significant issues may arise during the life of a campaign — issues that will need wise and careful resolution, often including board action. These include the following:

- *The unexpected mega-gift.* Does the school increase the dollar goal? Change the timetable? Make a public announcement even though the campaign is still in the quiet phase?

- *The unforeseen funding need.* How does the school prioritize the new need? Does it go into the campaign? Will it be pursued in a separate initiative?

- *The stalled nucleus phase.* Does the school go public with the campaign sooner? Lower the campaign goal? Fold in other purposes to boost campaign totals?

- *The nucleus fund goal is reached ahead of schedule.* Does the school increase the goal? Eliminate the public phase? Add future initiatives to the existing case?

These and other decision points are common in most campaigns. There are three critical principles to follow:

- Deliberate carefully about the right sequence, the right order, of campaign steps; keep the horse in front of the cart throughout the campaign.

- Keep the campaign calendar flexible, and always be mindful of the fatigue of lead volunteers and the broader school community.

- Understand that key decision points may emerge as planned, or suddenly, but at least one or two will confront every campaign.

THE CASE STATEMENT

The case statement provides the institution's opportunity to articulate campaign objectives for the school community and the compelling rationale that supports them. It should persuasively underscore the importance of the campaign and reflect institutional values and vision. It may also provide other campaign details, including ways to give, naming opportunities, the scale of gifts required, and contact information for key campaign leaders and staff. While traditionally considered a printed booklet, the campaign case may also be effectively expressed in other formats, including printed brochures, DVD and website presentations, and verbal communications by campaign volunteers and staff.

Volunteer and staff solicitors should take a copy of the case statement to every meeting with prospective donors. The document can be referred to during the visit and left behind for the prospect to review.

Although a finished, handsomely produced case statement is the desired outcome, the process of developing and refining it can be as important as the final product. Testing early drafts of the case statement with potential campaign leaders and prospects is an effective way to determine the most compelling campaign selling points and incorporate them into the case. The testing of the case is fundamentally important in reinforcing campaign objectives and rationale with campaign leaders and prospects and engendering campaign buy-in and ownership from key individuals early in the campaign.

Finally, it is important to recognize that a carefully written and designed case statement alone will not likely generate significant support from potential donors. Or, put another way, schools should not expect much of a return from sending a case statement with a return envelope to large groups of constituents. It is the personal contact of a volunteer or staff member, using the case statement in a dialogue with an engaged prospect, that is most compelling and persuasive.

LEADERSHIP AND VOLUNTEERS

Identifying and recruiting effective volunteers to leadership positions in the campaign is crucial. The ideal campaign chair (or co-chairs) has demonstrated leadership skills, is well respected and known in the community, is able to make a leadership gift, is comfortable soliciting gifts, and is passionate about achieving the campaign objectives. The chair or chairs will serve as campaign spokespersons to the board of trustees and work directly with the campaign staff through the various phases of the campaign. It is critical for the development office, the head of school, and the board chair to work together to identify top leadership candidates and then to determine the best approach to recruiting the potential campaign leaders. Assembling the leadership of the campaign takes time, but it is time well spent. A campaign will be successful if strong leadership is in place from the onset.

Volunteers are essential to almost any fund-raising venture, especially an independent school campaign. An ideal volunteer, like the leadership of the campaign, is respected in the community and comfortable soliciting gifts. Volunteers should know what will be expected of them (a job description is a good idea). They also need to be educated about the specifics of the case and about how to ask for support. It is important for all volunteers (even the most seasoned solicitor) to attend a training session. They will become more comfortable with the components of the case, and bringing them together will generate excitement about the school and will offer them the opportunity to learn from each other.

Managing and supporting a corps of volunteers takes a great deal of staff time. Volunteers need information and assistance on a regular basis. They need to be used respectfully: Do not overload volunteers with a large number of prospects; it is more effective to give them a small number of prospects (five to seven) to manage and complete before adding more to their caseload. Segmenting volunteers into various committees (e.g., leadership gift committee, major gift committee, parent gift committee), based on their giving ability and connection to the school, is an effective way to manage and meet their collective needs.

Many volunteers will not remain active throughout an entire multiyear campaign, so replenishing volunteer ranks should be an ongoing priority. Some may sign on for a limited amount of time or for a specific phase of the campaign. Also, the school's need for volunteers can change during the course of a campaign. Those who have already supported the campaign financially are an excellent source of potential volunteers. They are often the most enthusiastic and passionate campaign advocates and should be involved whenever possible.

Volunteers are a valuable asset that can ultimately transform a school's fund-raising efforts. Creating a structure in which peers are asking peers for support can change the culture of philanthropy at a school. Members of the community share the responsibility of supporting the school. Openness to talking about giving emerges, and a shift occurs in how people think about supporting the school. Individuals who once thought the school needed only annual giving may now embrace the idea of a larger gift given over multiple years. Ownership of the school's future success becomes a shared sentiment within the broader community.

CAMPAIGN STAFFING AND BUDGET

Campaign Staffing

A campaign provides the school with the opportunity to review its fund-raising resources and assess the staff's readiness to be successful in a major fund-raising initiative. New demands will be placed on the development office by a larger volunteer force, the cultivation and solicitation of many more major gift prospects, and the need for additional campaign communications and events. The school may wish to retain fund-raising counsel to conduct a comprehensive development office audit of current staffing and future needs. Many schools add staff to manage a campaign (i.e., campaign director or major gifts director) and administrative support for the increase in prospect data management, campaign reporting, pledge processing, and stewardship.

The head of school may also be dramatically affected by a campaign. The school head might devote as much as 50 percent of his or her job to fund raising. Most school heads play a lead role in donor cultivation and gift solicitation. Thus, many governing boards and administrative teams recognize the need for a school head to be away from campus and focused more externally. The school head may need education and training in order to play this lead campaign role effectively.

Lining up the appropriate advancement staff is vital. A campaign officer may manage a cadre of volunteers, oversee the campaign budget, report to the campaign leadership on a regular basis, and oversee the prospect pool. The number and geographical location of prospects and the number and effectiveness of volunteers will dictate the staff that is needed for a campaign. In larger campaigns, additional staffing may be needed, not only to support volunteers and to manage an increased prospect pool but also to actively solicit gifts. As the campaign moves into the public phase, many of the solicitations can fall on the staff as volunteer fatigue sets in or the volume of solicitations increases.

Some schools find outside fund-raising counsel to be a valuable investment during a campaign. Fund-raising counsel can serve as coach and advisor or be directly involved in the work of the campaign. Good consultants provide the school with a perspective from outside the immediate community. They can speak to trends at other schools and be the voice of experience throughout the independent school community.

Campaign Budget

To raise the increased funds sought in a major campaign, a school must upgrade fund-raising work and expertise. The cost of this increased activity should be as carefully planned as other aspects of the campaign. Often, a campaign consultant can help project expenses, but most independent schools invest an amount equal to 6 to 10 percent of the campaign goal, although budgets vary widely from school to school.

The key line items in traditional campaign budgets include the following:

- Staffing increases and realignments
- Case materials and campaign communications
- Events — kickoffs, cultivation gatherings, recognition dinners, etc.
- Data management and technology upgrades
- Electronic screening and outsourced donor research
- Individual prospect cultivation — travel, entertainment, solicitation expenses
- Fund-raising consultants and other outside vendors

Some schools expect the cost of campaign fund raising to be borne by the campaign revenues; others elect to pay for all fund-raising costs, including campaign expenses, through their annual operating budgets. In either scenario, campaign expenses are responsive to actual campaign progress. Thus, long-range cost projections for a large, multiyear campaign can be a challenge.

In the end, whether the school's approach to fund-raising expense is cost-efficiency, return on investment, or simply "it takes money to raise money," thoughtful budgeting, careful tracking of real campaign costs, and routinely shared information between the school's development and business functions are sound practices.

PROSPECTS

The Prospect Pool

Ultimately, donors determine the success of any fund-raising endeavor. The more an organization knows about its prospective donors, the more confidently it can establish and achieve campaign objectives. Identifying prospects — particularly leadership level prospects — and assessing their capacity and readiness to support institutional objectives should be an ongoing priority of any development effort. When preparing for a campaign, however, the school must have a thorough and systematic approach to this activity.

Early campaign attention should be given to identifying, cultivating, and assessing the likely support of a limited number of top major gift prospects. At the same time, the eventual success of most ambitious campaigns also depends on building and qualifying a broad pool of prospects at all giving levels. A careful assessment of this prospect pool helps establish appropriate campaign objectives; configure staff and volunteer duties; focus campaign resources on the most likely sources of support; and engender staff, volunteer, and community confidence in campaign success.

The lion's share of the campaign objectives will almost certainly be funded by those already known to the school: current and former trustees and other volunteers, previous major capital and annual fund donors, and known likely major prospects. These individuals are the critical core of the prospect pool. Therefore, the first priority is to systematically gather, update, and record information on the current giving capacity and readiness of these known campaign prospects.

It is worth emphasizing that previous major donors are the very best prospects for future gifts, provided that the school has effectively stewarded their past support, expressed its appreciation in multiple and ongoing ways, and cultivated relationships that go well beyond appreciation of their fund-raising potential. Recognizing the value (and the time and effort required) of thoughtfully stewarding the institution's relationship with major donors will affect not only the current campaign but any campaigns to follow.

Prospect Screening

Many reference materials, Internet research sites, and electronic screening services offer valuable information on prospects. Increasingly effective, these services help identify constituents who are not yet seen as viable prospects and inform and influence the ratings of known prospects. The school that uses outside screening services should be prepared to organize, store, and retrieve donor records with a reliable fund-raising software program.

Meanwhile, a helpful, readily available, and inexpensive source of information about prospects is the school community, members of whom know these individuals (and other prospects who may have been overlooked) and can provide invaluable information on their philanthropic priorities, giving capacity, inclination, and readiness to support a school's campaign.

A one-hour peer screening meeting with two or three well-connected volunteers (small groups are best) requires only a list of prospect names to review, staff guidance on the information sought, a reassurance of confidentiality, and a lot of note-taking by the staff member. This activity should go on throughout the campaign, as screening the same prospects with many small groups of volunteers at different points in the campaign will yield additional perspectives and increased confidence in the data gathered. Volunteer screeners should have the following questions in mind:

- Should this prospect be considered a campaign prospect?
- What are the factors — positive and negative — that might influence this prospect's support?
- What is known about this prospect's support of other organizations?
- Is this prospect a potential campaign volunteer?
- Who is the best person to approach this prospect?
- What is the prospect's estimated maximum giving capacity if the school were his or her highest philanthropic priority?
- How inclined and ready is this prospect to support the school's campaign objectives?
- What are the best case, worst case, and most likely case gifts from this prospect? (Some volunteer screeners may choose not to speculate to this degree and will defer to the development office to determine these estimates, based on all the information gathered.)
- Are there others who should be added to the list of prospects?

Assessing the Pool of Prospects

When maintained on a simple spreadsheet (Chart B), estimates of capacity and best, worst, and most likely gift can be sorted and tallied to provide essential information on the potential yield from the prospect pool.

CHART B

Name	Qualified?	Capacity	Best Case	Worst Case	Likely Gift
John and Mary Good	Yes	$100,000	$50,000	$10,000	$25,000
Art Dodger '49	Yes	$50,000	$10,000	$1,000	$5,000
Charlie Trueblue '76	Yes	$50,000	$50,000	$25,000	$50,000
Susan Rich But Distant	No	$500,000	$100,000	$0	$10,000
Total		$700,000	$210,000	$36,000	$90,000

Confidence in the estimates of potential support will vary from prospect to prospect, hence the "Qualified?" column in Chart B. Qualified prospects are those for whom similar estimates have been gathered from two or more sources (the more sources, the better). A prospect is not qualified if the projected giving estimates have come from only one source. Sorting on this column will distinguish estimates in which there is more confidence from those in which there is less.

The spreadsheet format in Chart B can be expanded to include other data important to a given institution or campaign — constituency, trustee, class year, assigned campaign volunteer, readiness to be asked, etc. Even this simple format can be used to identify those most likely to give at a leadership level, those with the greatest capacity (who should be the focus of careful cultivation), the number of prospects at a given level, the confidence level of giving projections, and the total capacity and likely support from a selected group of constituents — or the entire pool.

Another consideration that should be factored into an estimate of the aggregate capacity of a prospect pool is the fact that only a fraction of the prospects rated at a given level will actually support the campaign at that level. A common rule of thumb is that three prospects at a given level are needed to secure one contribution. For instance, if 15 prospects are qualified at the $100,000 level, approximately five will actually give at that level, and the others will give less or not at all. The more that is known about the capacity, inclination, and readiness of individual prospects, the more accurate the projected estimates are likely to be and the greater the yield will be at any giving level.

A prospect pool will continue to evolve throughout a campaign. Individuals will move on and off the prospect list; giving estimates will be adjusted up and down, based on newly acquired information; and prospects will make commitments (or choose not to) and be removed from the active prospect list. A well-managed and updated prospect list will, at any point in the campaign, provide the best possible estimate of potential future support, based on the remaining prospects.

Most development officers have experienced the empty feeling that follows the inevitable question, "How much can we raise, and how do you know?" Predicting the behavior of individual prospects — who will contribute at what level — will make even the most seasoned fund raisers weak in the knees. Predicting the behavior of a pool of prospects, however, is less problematic, as the highs and lows are balanced by many others whose support will be more in line with giving projections. Even though it is still an imprecise business, systematically assembling and assessing a pool of well-screened and qualified prospects remains the most essential task in setting a realistic goal and conducting a successful capital campaign.

PARTING THOUGHTS ON CAMPAIGN CONDUCT

Here are some points to keep in mind.

- Everything will take longer than expected. Developing a case statement; recruiting volunteers; arranging meetings with prospects; deciding if, when, and how much they will give — this all takes time. Be patient, build extra time into the plan, and don't be discouraged.

- There will be surprises — good and bad. Gifts will come from unexpected sources, and other "sure bets" will give less than expected. Don't be influenced too much by either.

- A small number of volunteers (and staff) will raise the majority of the funds. Many volunteers will help, but a small group of committed core leaders will cultivate and solicit most key prospects. Considerable staff energies should be focused on supporting these critically important volunteers.

- Focus on prospects with supportive inclinations. Be pleasantly persistent, but recognize that some prospects are not ever going to give, or give what is hoped for. Move on.

- It's about the big gifts. With increasingly greater percentages of campaign goals being funded by those giving at the very highest levels, identifying these individuals and developing strategies and opportunities to engage them in the campaign is essential.

- Don't get lost in the parties and brochures — visit prospects. Successful major gift fund raising is about individual relationships and face-to-face contact with prospects.

- The vast majority of the funds raised will come from prospects already known to the school. There will be exceptions, but schools should not expect currently unknown or unconnected prospects to provide a significant portion of the campaign goal.

- Expect summer doldrums. Plan to accommodate reduced campaign activity and progress during the summer months when many prospects and volunteers are traveling, vacationing, and otherwise less focused on school.

- Engaging top prospects in the school's vision and plans is a fundamental campaign priority. Achieving campaign objectives must be *their* project and *their* passion.

- It's not about the campaign. Few donors are inspired to give generously in order to achieve a campaign's financial goals. Focus on what the funding will make possible for students, teachers, and the community.

- Engage and ask!

CONCLUSION

Capital campaigns provide opportunities to substantially increase the support from all school constituencies and to achieve exciting institutional objectives that would otherwise be impossible. Successful campaigns provide other important benefits to the institution as well, including the following:

- A culture of increased philanthropic support of the school

- An infrastructure of staff, volunteers, and activities — and a larger base of donors and prospective donors — that will sustain high levels of support long after the campaign

- Increased institutional visibility, stature, and momentum, which will positively influence student admission, faculty recruitment, and school pride in general

Finally, no matter the size of the institution, the goal, or the development office, successful campaigns are the coming together of a compelling need, those with the financial capacity to give, and individuals who can effectively bring the two together. Campaigns transform institutions and influence generations of students. They provide those involved — school heads, trustees, development officers, and volunteers — with a wonderful opportunity to reveal new horizons and make a lasting difference in the lives of children. Few endeavors are more rewarding or more important.

CHAPTER 8

Planned Giving: The Road to Larger Gifts

By Herbert P. Soles

"I cannot begin to tell you how important The Reynolds School has been in my life. So much of my success I owe to the education I received there and to the many teachers who believed in me and inspired me to be the best I could be. I want to give back. I want others to have the same opportunity I had. I'd really love to be able to establish an endowed scholarship fund at Reynolds, but unfortunately I have too many assets tied up in real estate at this time."— Mr. Goodwill

How often have development directors heard prospects discuss personal circumstances similar to those of Mr. Goodwill? Mr. Goodwill wants to give. He wants to help. However, he does not believe he can afford to make the commitment. What do fund raisers need to know in order to remove that doubt and to offer Mr. Goodwill and so many others like him the fulfillment of their dreams?

Planned giving often leads to a more successful solicitation. It gives prospects the ability to make larger gifts than they believed were possible.

Imagine asking a loyal alumnus the following questions.

"Would you be willing and able to make a major gift if you could …

- receive income for the rest of your life?"

- avoid capital gains taxes?"

- dispose of problem assets?"

- receive tax-free income?"

- receive a partial tax deduction now?"

"What if you could take advantage of all of the above?"

The ability of a solicitor to engage in such a dialogue with a qualified prospect can turn a generous person who has lost interest in giving due to a perceived lack of resources into a donor who can help change the life of a school.

A basic understanding of a few planned giving concepts can enable a development director to continue this conversation — a conversation that could very well lead to a substantial gift. Remember, it is not necessary to be a financial planning or tax expert to enjoy such success. The development officer only needs basic information about some of the gift vehicles through which donors can expand their giving potential.

WHY PLANNED GIVING IS ESSENTIAL

Almost all of today's largest gifts include some component of planned giving. Sophisticated donors may hesitate to write a check for a six- or seven-figure gift because they want to use the best tax-wise techniques to maximize the benefits of their generosity.

Fund raisers are much more successful if they have a working knowledge of some of these tax-beneficial techniques. At the same time, most development directors are neither lawyers nor financial planners and therefore must not appear to practice law by advising prospects about ways to design their gifts. Instead, suggesting where they might find additional information and advice can lead prospects down the path to a major gift.

A qualified major gift prospect should have the following three attributes:

1. The ability to give

2. A commitment to the school or project

3. A track record of giving

Development officers spend significant time and resources on cultivation and stewardship in order to increase both donors' commitments and gift levels. But often it is not the prospect's *capacity* to give that stands in the way but rather the prospect's *perception* of that capacity.

Many prospects simply do not realize that the school can help them create a plan that benefits both the school and the donor. It is critically important that prospects view development directors as advocates trying to help them achieve what they previously did not think was possible. That is relationship fund raising at its very best.

PLANNED GIVING DEFINED

Traditionally, fund raisers have tried to match the right prospect with the right institutional need, resulting in a gift to the school. Planned giving, however, adds another dimension. It matches the right prospect with the school's need *and* with a certain asset and type of gift vehicle that creates a benefit for both the donor and the school.

Traditional fund raising: Donor + need = Benefit for the school
Planned giving: Donor + need + asset and gift vehicle = Benefit for the school and the donor

Assets that have been used for planned gifts include the following:
- Appreciated securities
- Family business interests and closely held stock
- Bonds
- Real estate
- Qualified retirement plan benefits
- Life insurance
- Tangible personal property
- Intangible personal property

Gift vehicles include the following:
- Outright gifts
- Bequests

- Trusts that distribute income to the school for a period of years with the remaining assets going to one or more designees of the donor at the end of the trust period

- Trusts that distribute income to the donor or a person designated by the donor for a period of years with the remaining assets going to the school at the end of the trust period

Often, development directors are overwhelmed by the myriad of opportunities and will therefore do nothing. Though it is useful to know as much as possible about these opportunities, it is by no means necessary to promote all of the plans available.

THE BEQUEST: THE FOUNDATION OF ALL PLANNED GIVING PROGRAMS

Every planned giving program should begin with a focus on bequests. They are the easiest planned gift to obtain, and they require little or no technical skill.

The importance of securing bequests cannot be overstated. It is the planned gift of choice for most prospects and the gift that they are most likely to know about and understand. Every competent attorney, during a will preparation discussion, should ask clients if they wish to support a charity. It is not unusual to read about a person or organization receiving a sizable inheritance or gift through a bequest. In fact, bequests are the single largest source of endowment gifts from individuals, and a bequest often provides the largest gift a school will receive.

Never Underestimate the Value of a Bequest

Many charitable organizations focus their entire planned giving efforts on bequest promotion alone. Even though the final gift arrangement requires the service of an attorney, the initial discussions can be with the school. The suggestion that a bequest could be a viable gift option may open a prospect's eyes to a larger potential gift than he or she had initially considered. Perhaps a combined gift of cash and a bequest would be even more exciting. For example, a prospect might be asked, "Would you consider providing an annual $5,000 partial scholarship for a qualified student in need? In addition, you could create an endowed fund and ensure this wonderful support, forever, by leaving the school $100,000 in your will." During such a conversation, immediate support is requested, and the prospect's sights for the future are raised as well.

There are several options that a donor may use. He or she may choose a specific bequest of cash, securities, real estate, or tangible personal property. For example, the donor may leave "100 shares of Microsoft stock to the endowed scholarship fund" or "My beach house in Boca Raton, Florida, to the school's music department."

Or the donor may choose to leave a percentage of his or her estate. The percentage can be based on the gross or net assets of the estate. For example, "I leave 5 percent of my gross estate to The Reynolds School," or "After all expenses, debts, and taxes are paid, I leave The Reynolds School 10 percent of my net assets."

Finally, the donor can leave his or her residual estate, that which is left after all other obligations have been met. For example, "The Reynolds School is to receive 50 percent of the entire rest, residue, and remainder of my estate." This is an excellent option for those prospects who have concerns about whether or not they have adequately provided for their heirs. In this case, the donor takes care of family and friends first. The school receives what is left.

Every donor who commits to a bequest is indicating that he or she cares deeply about the school's mission and goals. Therefore, all promised bequests should be welcomed and honored no matter how long the school must wait to receive the funds. When properly cultivated over time, these prospects, who are signaling their strong interest in the school and their sincere desire to help, may upgrade their commitments to a lifetime gift. Even though a school may not receive the financial benefit for a long time, from the donor's point of view, a bequest is a meaningful current commitment. Thus, it is important to treat a bequest notification as a gift deserving immediate gratitude, recognition, and praise.

THREE ASSETS TO SEEK

Independent schools most frequently seek three assets:

1. Appreciated securities

2. Appreciated real estate

3. Qualified retirement plan benefits

No matter where the Dow Jones Industrial Average may be and no matter how much pessimism there is on Wall Street, there will always be wealthy prospects who have appreciated securities and who do not want to pay a capital gains tax.

Why are gifts of appreciated securities so beneficial to a prospect?

When a donor makes a gift of an appreciated security (stock held for more than one year) to a qualified charity, he or she may take a tax deduction for the full fair market value of the security on the day of the gift. In addition, the donor will not be required to pay a capital gains tax for the excess of the value of the stock over his or her cost. Many donors of appreciated securities view this result as a double tax deduction.

However, in order to avoid capital gains taxes, the donor must transfer the stock directly to the school, rather than selling the stock and donating the proceeds. The determination of the fair market value is easy. Simply have a broker provide the average between the high and low of the stock on the day of the gift and multiply the average times the number of shares given.

Real estate is often a choice asset to donate because it provides options for the donor.

The donor of real estate can receive the same advantages as the donor of appreciated securities: (1) a tax deduction for the full fair market value and (2) the avoidance of capital gains taxes. However, appreciated real estate can be given to the school in its entirety, or the donor can give an undivided interest. Furthermore, a donor can give the school a residential property and retain use during his or her lifetime or for a period of years, with full ownership passing to the school at a designated future time.

Gifts of appreciated real estate are somewhat more complex. First, the value of the gift must be established by a qualified appraiser. Legal fees for the transfer, as well as who pays these fees, must be determined. Never shortcut the process and accept property without completing a full title search. It may also be prudent to have an outside expert make a personal visit and prepare an evaluation of the property. There are charities that accept gifts of real estate only after an environmental impact study has been done. It is wise to establish a set of written policies to establish standards for real estate gift acceptance in advance.

Recently, with more of the boomer generation approaching retirement age, increased interest and attention have been given to gifts created through retirement plans. Many successful people made contributions to Individual Retirement Accounts (IRAs) early in their careers. As their wealth grows, these accounts are no longer as critical to their retirement strategy as they were earlier in life. Placing the school as a death-time beneficiary of their IRAs might be a good use of an asset (less the mandatory distributions that they must take after age 70½) that is no longer as important in their own long-term financial picture.

FOUR GIFT VEHICLES THAT GIVE BACK TO THE DONOR

A charitable remainder trust is especially appealing to the potential donor who has a strong desire to retain income. In most cases, the donor funds the trust with highly appreciated property, usually securities or real estate. The trustee then pays income to the donor or a designated individual for the remainder of his or her life (or a predetermined period of years). At the conclusion of the trust, all remaining assets go to the school.

Charitable remainder trusts usually take one of two forms. The *charitable remainder unitrust (CRUT)* pays the beneficiary a predetermined percentage of the declared value of the trust's assets each year on the anniversary of the trust's creation. Any earnings or appreciation of the trust's assets in excess of the annual disbursement to the beneficiary remains in the trust and thus provides the opportunity for the principal to grow, resulting in an increased annual payment. For those who are not confident in continued inflation, another choice is available. The *charitable remainder annuity trust (CRAT)* pays the beneficiary a set amount each year, predetermined at the creation of the trust.

Both trusts potentially provide the donor with income for life, some capital gains tax deferral, removal of selected assets from his or her estate, partial tax-free income, and a one-time upfront tax deduction. Do not forget the most important benefit: The donor knows that the school will receive a significant gift in the future.

The *charitable gift annuity* is one of the oldest and most popular planned gift vehicles. Gone are the legal complications that donors often associate with charitable remainder trusts. Because it is not a trust, it does not require a trustee. A charitable gift annuity can be established with a simple one-page contract. Here is how it works: The donor gives the school cash or securities, and the school agrees, by contract, to give the donor a certain amount of money (an annuity) for the remainder of the life of the donor or an individual designated by the donor. Most schools use the recommended rates provided by the American Council on Gift Annuities (ACGA) to determine the annual amount to be paid.

Because this gift vehicle is a simple contract between the school and the donor, gone, too, are the usual fees and expenses associated with trusts. Charitable gift annuities can be established with more modest gifts. Whereas most charitable remainder trusts are for $100,000 or more, charitable gift annuity levels can be as low as $2,500.

The gift annuity has another interesting feature. Should the donor wish to defer payments from the school until a later time, the rate of return is increased. The *deferred charitable gift annuity* can be very helpful to young donors seeking tax-wise retirement plans because they can put off receipt of the distributions until retirement.

Some independent schools choose not to offer gift annuities because of certain onerous regulations by state insurance commissions. Do not prematurely dismiss this potentially valuable option because it could have significant benefits for donors. First, refer to the ACGA's website (*www.acga-web.org*) to learn about the requirements of individual states.

FIVE KEY COMPONENTS OF A SUCCESSFUL PLANNED GIVING PROGRAM

The following five vital ingredients are found in all thriving planned giving programs whether a school is creating its first planned giving initiative or improving an existing program.

1. Leadership commitment is essential.

Begin with the head of school, board chair, and board development committee chair. It is rare for a program to succeed if these leaders do not fully back the effort. However, if they believe that the potential of planned giving is worth the investment of patience, focus, and school resources, others will follow their lead. The business manager and board finance committee chair are also important members of the planned giving team. At times, it will be necessary for the business manager to help administer various gift vehicles. A wise development director seeks the understanding, cooperation, and collaboration of the school's financial leadership.

2. Program structure and organization need not be complex.

The creation of a few volunteer committees will be useful. First, establish a Professional Advisory Board. This committee's responsibility is to provide technical support for the professional staff. The membership should include trust and estate attorneys, certified financial planners, bank officers, certified life insurance agents, and other technical experts who understand that they represent the school and therefore cannot also represent the donors. The members should be available, individually, when needed. A Planned Giving Committee should be composed of those who have already made a planned gift and who want to help market the benefits of such a gift to others. This team of witnesses can be most effective. Finally, a board-appointed Gift Acceptance and Recognition Committee has the responsibility of creating and interpreting written Gift Acceptance and Recognition Policies. Its first responsibility should be to write policies for board approval. The policies should state specifically how the committee, on behalf of the board, will cope with unusual gift circumstances and how it will respond to requested exceptions to the policies. Additional information is available from the National Committee on Planned Giving (*www.ncpg.org*) and the ACGA.

3. Education of the school community about planned giving techniques and opportunities should be a major priority.

It is much easier to sell planned giving to an educated and sophisticated audience of believers than to a confused and suspicious set of naysayers. There are clear, well-written texts available to begin a personal education. Many communities have planned giving study groups that provide networking and study opportunities at all levels of experience. Planned giving consultants offer a wide variety of brochures, newsletters, and seminars. There are good user-friendly software programs that can help staff members understand and design planned gift examples. Information and knowledge should be shared with staff and volunteers. Presentations should be made to board committees, parent organizations, and alumni groups. The successful development officer must be creative and look for new ways to spread the word. However, development officers should share with planned gift prospects "what some donors like you have done" and not "what you should do."

4. Marketing and communication of planned giving are limited only by the budget and by the professional development staff's imagination. Most planned giving vehicles afford interesting opportunities that prospects may not have considered. An informative brochure with detailed explanations and examples of common gift vehicles can be useful. Listing ways of giving with short, simple definitions and concise explanations in the annual report can create interest as well as help break up long, sometimes boring, lists of donor names. Many schools find it effective to place a box that prospects can check to request planned giving information at the bottom of their annual giving pledge cards.

A feature article in the school's magazine, newsletter, or annual report about a commitment from a recent donor can provide inspiration. When donors share what motivated them or why a particular vehicle was especially attractive, others pay attention. Testimonial articles are even more effective when they are accompanied by a sidebar that explains in nontechnical language how the gift works. Referring to the article can be valuable in subsequent conversations with targeted prospects. If the gift is of significant size, it would be worth the cost to mail a special announcement that gives more attention to the gift and the method of giving.

Many consulting firms offer a wide array of easily understood pamphlets and educational newsletters that can be adapted and personalized to fit a school's needs and culture. Some firms also produce interactive components to the school's website with links to detailed, informative articles.

Never forget that word of mouth is indispensable. If the program is active and the professional staff is responsive, the word will spread. Success will build on success. Still, no matter how much is spent or how clever the promotion, diligent and immediate followup by the professional staff is essential if the program is to succeed.

5. Establishment of a solid bequest program is crucial.

Many charitable organizations concentrate their attention on bequests alone. Many studies have provided shocking statistics that show how few people have current, updated wills. Therefore, a financial planning seminar hosted by the school and directed to a target audience offers a helpful service as well as an example of how the school can be included in an estate plan. Most schools have an attorney or financial planner in their communities who can provide presentations to a luncheon group or at an evening gathering. Consider a series of financial planning seminars that cover other topics, such as retirement planning and current tax issues. All such sessions should be nontechnical and geared to donor motivations and benefits rather than focused on the details of planned giving vehicles. Planning, organizing, and presenting seminars can be an appropriate activity for the Planned Giving Committee or Professional Advisory Board.

An excellent way to steward the planned gift donor is to invite him or her to join a special legacy or heritage society. Most schools have very liberal membership requirements. They simply ask society members to state in writing that they have included the school in their estate plans. Other schools ask that more detailed applications be completed. However, there should never be a minimum gift requirement. The purpose of a society is to recognize the donor and to celebrate a special commitment. The fund-raising program will profit from having an enthusiastic group of satisfied patrons extolling this unique way of contributing. The school will benefit by helping ensure that revocable gifts remain intact until maturity. Often, society members will respond to effective stewardship by increasing their initial commitments.

MR. GOODWILL MAKES A PLANNED GIFT

The Reynolds School development director was eager to help Mr. Goodwill fulfill his dream of a lasting gift. After a series of thoughtful conversations with the head of The Reynolds School, Mr. Goodwill decided that he wanted to create an endowed scholarship fund. But how could he afford it? After reading an article in the *Alumni Magazine* about a classmate who had established an endowed fund for faculty salaries using real estate assets, he became intrigued by the possibilities. His discussions with The Reynolds School development director excited him even more as he learned about a tax-wise method to make a very large gift that would also address a number of his financial concerns.

Mr. Goodwill, age 50, owned a rental property that was highly appreciated, yet produced less than a 2 percent return on its $500,000 value. He was especially concerned that future increases in maintenance and repair costs could reduce his income. His CPA warned that the property might develop a negative cash flow.

After consulting with his attorney, Mr. Goodwill placed the property in a charitable remainder unitrust and appointed his bank as trustee. The trust provided for an annual distribution to Mr. Goodwill of 5 percent of its value. The trustee then sold the property and invested the proceeds in a balanced portfolio of stocks and bonds. On the first anniversary of the trust's creation, Mr. Goodwill would begin to receive an annual distribution check from the trustee.

Good news came from his CPA when she estimated the results:

- His first check would be $25,000. With an estimated annual net growth of 3 percent after Mr. Goodwill received his 5 percent payments, he should receive approximately $32,000 in year 10 and $42,000 in year 20.

- Capital gains would be spread over a number of years.

- He would receive an immediate one-time tax deduction in excess of $100,000.

- He would dispose of his problem property.

- If the anticipated growth in value occurred, The Reynolds School would receive more than $1 million on his death.

A feature article in the *Alumni Magazine* described Mr. Goodwill's plan to create an endowed scholarship fund. He stated that he was so pleased with the outcome that he would also make additional annual gifts during his lifetime to provide scholarship aid for at least one student each year. Soon after publication of the article, he received a thank-you note from a trustee. The trustee's note included the following paragraph:

> Not only have you made a generous commitment to The Reynolds School but you have also set a wonderful example that your classmates and many others will follow in future years. We will always think of you with gratitude and pride knowing that deserving students will be attending The Reynolds School because of your loyalty, thoughtfulness, and creativity.

CHAPTER 9

The Essentials of Alumni Relations

By Harold Brown

"Love all of the alumni all of the time!"

The new alumni* director sat in his office on his third day at The Reynolds School. His first two days had been spent "in training" with his predecessor. The training had been intense and much too short. The two days included an introduction to "key people" on campus, an exhaustive review of the department files, and meetings with his new colleagues. After day two, his mind was spinning with reunion schedules and volunteer meetings. He wondered if he would ever be able to remember all of the alumni names and their classes.

The new director found himself pondering one question: What is the primary objective of alumni relations? Is it to create fun and memorable events and experiences for the alumni? Is it to be a resource for alumni, a place to handle alumni inquiries and respond to alumni requests? Or is it essentially what one of his friends described as "a setup for fund raising"?

His thoughts were interrupted by H. Henry Russell, a retired, 80-year-old

---

* For simplicity, all references in this chapter are to alumni and an alumnus, but the advice applies to alumnae and an alumna as well.

gentleman who had spent 49 years at the school as a student, teacher, coach, admissions officer, and alumni director.

"I heard that you were settling into your new job and I thought I'd come by to wish you luck and share a thought or two with you," Russell said as he took a seat. "Would you like to know the most important thing to remember about your job?

Stunned by this question, the director answered with more enthusiasm than he wanted to show, "Yes!"

Russell leaned forward in his chair, fixed his eyes on the new director, and said,

"Well, most of the people in this building love some of the alumni some of the time. But you must love all of the alumni all of the time. That is the essence of your job, making sure that all of the alumni feel valued and respected by Reynolds, not for what they can contribute financially or otherwise but just because they are Reynolds alumni.

He paused to let the words sink in, adding, "This work is simple but not easy. Keep it simple and work hard."

With that, H. Henry Russell stood up, shook the new director's hand, and left the office.

There are two important elements of this primary objective of loving all the alumni all the time:

- Commitment to a lifelong relationship with alumni
- The quality of the relationship between alumni and the school

COMMITMENT TO A LIFELONG RELATIONSHIP

Commitment to a lifelong relationship between alumni and their school requires a certain level of affinity and engagement. Everyone understands that alumni are alumni until death.

However, that only addresses one side of the relationship equation. What is the school willing to do in order to develop an ongoing relationship with its alumni? Is it reasonable to strive to engage all of the alumni all of the time? Of course it is. If teachers strive to engage all students during all the days of their relationship with the school, then the alumni relations staff should strive to engage all alumni throughout their lives.

The thought of forming lifelong relationships with all alumni in this manner can be daunting. Maintaining lifelong relationships between alumni and their alma mater requires effort, creativity, and resolve. Independent schools have limited resources. Most alumni relations offices are staffed by one to three people who play several roles including fund raiser, event planner, parent relations officer, and communications officer.

Schools often attempt to resolve this array of competing roles by focusing on fund solicitation at the expense of other alumni relations activities. The unintended impression that this strategy may convey to alumni is that their alma maters only care about them when they want something, usually money. Larger alumni relations operations can also convey this impression when their schools allow fund solicitation activities to dominate communications and other interactions with alumni. In either situation, the potential of establishing a quality lifelong relationship with alumni is diminished.

THE QUALITY OF THE RELATIONSHIP

The best relationships between people have at their core a mutual commitment to the interests of the individuals involved. Respect, integrity, and trust are present in all quality relationships.

The relationships between a school and its alumni must embody these same attributes. All alumni relations professionals (indeed, all advancement professionals) should strive to treat alumni with even more care and respect than they may receive in return. The importance of this principle cannot be overstated. It applies equally to alumni who are generous with their resources (financial and time) as well as to those who contribute little of these resources or none at all.

In such a relationship, the school respects the whole alumnus — successes, failures, and concerns. The school seeks and values the alumnus's feedback and involvement and readily acknowledges these contributions. The alumnus does not need to pass any tests to win the approval of the school, but automatically feels respected and is confident of the school's goodwill and integrity. The opportunity to participate in the life of the school or contribute to its mission is an irresistible invitation to an alumnus and serves as a testament of his value to his alma mater. When alumni have such a relationship with their alma mater, they are motivated to respond to the school's appeal for valuable resources (time and money) because of the underlying trust that has been developed.

THE WORK IS SIMPLE BUT NOT EASY

Alumni relations work is hard, especially in independent schools. The attitude that the alumnus holds toward the school is based on the combination of experiences of the student years, which can span the grades from kindergarten through high school. When one considers the range of emotions and experiences that students encounter during those years — experiences with teachers, administrators, and staff; their sense of accomplishment and achievement; the ebb and flow of self-esteem; and their relationships with peers — the difficulty of the task becomes apparent, almost palpable. Alumni form strong opinions about their schools long before their first encounter with the alumni relations office. In addition, the manner in which independent schools are portrayed in the media or by friends and relatives can influence how the institution is perceived by its alumni.

Moreover, every independent school in America is competing for the time and attention of its alumni with colleges and universities, medical organizations, community-based organizations, religious organizations, career demands, and family.

Given all of these challenges, how does a school achieve its objective of "loving all the alumni all the time?" Here are 10 suggestions:

1. Begin cultivating the relationship before alumni graduate, the earlier the better.

Some schools begin the process as early as the primary years (K–3) with, for example, a student-to-alumnus pen pal program, student-prepared care packages to college-age alumni during their exam weeks, or activities during Halloween. An invitation to an alumnus to participate in school activities with students is irresistible! It affirms the alumnus's value to the school, and it produces a memorable experience that will enrich the relationship.

2. Keep the focus of the relationship on the school.

The alumni relations professional is a liaison between the school and its alumni. A common pitfall for the alumni director is to allow personal relationships with alumni to take priority over the relationship between the alumnus and the school. This places the school in a vulnerable position, especially if the staffer changes jobs or leaves. It may also inhibit the director's ability to present controversial school policies in an appropriate manner to alumni. As a liaison, the director's proper role is to present school policies to alumni and report their reactions to those policies to the school.

3. Involve all members of the school community in building alumni relationships.

Everyone in the school should be involved in alumni relations work. This includes the school head, staff, faculty, and students. Alumni are pleased to see former teachers and current students. Class reunions, regional events, and student performances all provide excellent opportunities for quality interactions between alumni and other members of the school community. This will serve to increase and diversify the number of alumni interactions with the school as well as to leverage the impact of the alumni relations team.

4. Set goals for engaging alumni.

There is a misconception that alumni relations work is too soft to measure. To be sure, the success of alumni relations is not as easy to measure as the success of fund raising. However, there are many indicators of alumni affinity and engagement. Attendance at events, first-time attendees, campus visits, volunteers, participation in the annual fund, and legacy students' applications are just a few. Surveys are also good tools to assess alumni affinity. A school's commitment to building and maintaining quality relationships with its alumni is directly related to its willingness to define and to set relevant goals in this area.

5. Be attentive and sensitive to the changing work/life patterns of the alumni body.

Alumni are living longer. They are more health conscious. Their workday may be longer. They have less discretionary time. Therefore, schools should plan activities that complement work/life patterns. For example, since many alumni may no longer have time for sit-down dinners, plan receptions that are less formal and have shorter presentations. This will provide greater opportunities for networking at a fraction of the cost. Rising transportation costs and declining discretionary time are negatively impacting attendance at class reunions, especially at boarding schools where a larger percentage of alumni live considerable distances from the school. To accommodate these trends, many schools are planning mini-class reunions in cities where large numbers of alumni live. In addition, schools have added programs for children, spouses, and partners to permit alumni to attend a reunion without sacrificing time with their families. Because older alumni may be crying out for opportunities to connect and reminisce, consider a 70th reunion. Don't be afraid to experiment!

6. Keep alumni informed about the school.

School magazines and electronic newsletters are excellent communication tools to keep alumni informed about the life of the school. They are also excellent affinity builders. These publications should feature stories about the students, faculty, and staff. They should also include lots of photos. Electronic newsletters are very popular because their dynamic nature provides opportunities to engage alumni in real time through such devices as surveys and blogs. Electronic communications can be expensive, but they are indispensible today since people are more apt to read e-mail than U.S. mail.

7. Help alumni build and maintain relationships with other alumni.

This is one of the most powerful ways to strengthen the ties between alumni and the school. The dynamic of alumni-to-alumni interaction can build school affinity dramatically. Here are a few instruments that facilitate networking among alumni:

- Online directories provide ways for alumni to locate each other as well as to update their own contact information.

- Online social networking communities are powerful tools for connecting alumni to each other, but these communications present interesting challenges for schools. Products like Facebook® are rapidly replacing e-mail as the communications medium of choice for alumni, especially younger alumni. Since young alumni seldom use the U.S. mail, schools must find ways either to participate in these online communities or to build alternatives.

- Mentoring programs create opportunities for alumni to counsel other alumni regarding career and other life issues.

- Volunteer leadership gatherings, phonathons, reunion committees, and regional associations all strengthen the ties among alumni, which, in turn, strengthen the relationship between the alumni and the school.

8. Acquire knowledge and understanding of the culture and history of the school.

The best sources for this information are founding documents, retired faculty, the school magazine, student publications, and other material produced by members of the school family over time. Faculty and student organization meetings provide insights into the teaching style and governance of the school as well as the culture of the student body. The insights and information provide a strong foundation for conversations with alumni and place the alumni director in a good position to build bridges between the school the alumni attended and the school as it is today.

9. The integrity of the alumni relations staff is paramount.

The alumni relations professional should be dependable and honest. The alumnus needs to be able to count on the information and promises provided by the staff. If the alumni director does not know the answer to a question, it's best to admit it and promise to get an answer in a reasonable timeframe. Through honest interactions, the alumni director will win the respect and trust of the alumni.

10. The school should strive to retain high-quality, long-term alumni relations professionals.

Long tenure in the alumni office conveys institutional stability and provides continuity for the program. A familiar face reassures alumni of the school's commitment to them and promotes a sense of family. Alumni are impressed when employees form long-lasting relationships with their school.

THE
PEOPLE

CHAPTER 10

Key Relationships in a Development Program

By Peter D. Relic

I n an ideal world, the following statements are always true: "The director of development is a full member of the head's administrative team, participating in all deliberations and decisions." "The director of development works hand-in-glove with the board's development committee." "The head of school and the director are on the same page in all aspects of fund raising." Unfortunately, that is not always the case.

A development director recently said, "The head of school walked into my office just as we were set to launch this year's annual fund. All smiles and cordiality, he explained the goals for a new capital campaign that he and the trustees had just drawn up. A $40 million goal and my office had had no input. 'Go to it!' he intoned."

Another development officer said, "I am considered a member of the head's administrative council and I am supposed to be knowledgeable about the institutional needs and the curriculum and programs of the school, but I never attend meetings at which the division heads discuss what's going on."

These examples are extreme, but the reality is clear: It is important for all participants in a development program to establish clear procedures for working together and to follow these procedures in a consistent and collegial manner.

Here are four important facts:

- Development is a profession. The field of institutional advancement has become so complex and so far-reaching in its impact that the director of the program must be professional and must be acknowledged as such.

- Within the development office, collaboration and cooperation are essential. There should be ample opportunities for the staff to brainstorm and to participate in decision-making.

- The director of development must be able to speak with knowledge and authority about the school. Therefore, he or she should be a full participating member of the head of school's administrative council.

- The development staff must have a passion for the mission of the school. It is its responsibility to publicize and to promote that mission throughout the community.

With those facts in mind, here are the 13 relationships that are key to development success:

1. The director of development and the head of school

The director can succeed only if the head of school has trust, faith, and confidence in him or her as a professional and as a colleague. Together, they should be a close, two-person team communicating frequently and working together well. Some heads spend 50 percent of their time working on development with the full board and the development committee, with major prospects and donors, and with alumni across the nation and around the world.

2. The director of development and the development office staff

The director of development leads the staff and sets the tone. Especially because the pressures on and the expectations of the office are significant, he or she should create a culture of respect, civility, sensitivity, and pride. In a top-notch development office:

- There is an ethic of hard work.

- All staff members contribute ideas, have responsibility for programs, and are willing to be held accountable.

- Successes are recognized and celebrated.
- The staff is visible and appreciated throughout the school.

3. The director of development and the head of school's administrative team

The director of development should be a full participating member of the head of school's administrative council, which includes the assistant head of school, the business officer, division heads, the admissions director, the athletic director, and the director of communications and technology as well.

It is essential for a director of development to be aware of the latest plans for curricular enhancement, the growing controversy among league schools about athletic recruitment, the news that two teachers have just been awarded summer Fulbright fellowships, and the fact that endowment income is inadequate to underwrite arts center maintenance and repair. In addition, other administrators benefit from the insights and perspective that the director of development provides.

4. The director of development and the business manager

The director of development and the business manager should be close colleagues. The business manager has the expertise and responsibilities that are vital to the effective functioning of the development office. The two staffs should think and comport themselves as members of the same team. The computer systems and technologies in the two offices should be compatible and, at all times, their gift accounting records should be the same.

5. The director of development and the development committee of the board

The director of development and the board's development committee should be a team, focusing together on solicitations, major donor cultivation and leadership gifts, tax-exempt bonds and changing tax laws, feasibility studies, and naming opportunities. Fortunately, most school heads and trustees understand that the director of development must participate in discussions about the annual fund, capital campaigns, endowments, and planned gifts. No head of school should feel threatened by the interaction of the development director and the trustees.

6. The director of development and the full board of trustees

Beyond the director's ongoing work with the development committee, he or she should also attend meetings of the full board. One director of development reports, "I have never attended a board meeting — never. The head simply does not want me there." To isolate the development director from trustees, many of whom may be major donors, is unwise. Instead, the head of school, the director of development, and the chairs of the board and the campaign committee should collaborate on reports to the board about the school's fund-raising successes and challenges.

7. The director of development and alumni

Alumni are the one constituency that has a lifetime relationship with the school. Therefore, the director of development needs to know them and communicate with them, and alumni need to understand that the development director is a capable, dedicated administrator at the school they love. The director of development should be able to greet by name alumni who attend school plays, concerts, and athletic events. And the development staff should interact often and personally with alumni who are key prospects or generous donors. The relationship between development and alumni must be close and cooperative, even though, too often, the alumni office is in the basement of the school's oldest building far away from the development staff.

8. The director of development and the faculty

Imagine two scenarios: one in which the faculty appreciates and supports the development program and another in which the faculty has little knowledge or understanding of development. In the second case, why should 100 percent of the faculty participate in the annual fund? It is up to the director of development to communicate with faculty members, to teach them about the work of the development staff and the importance of the development program.

9. The director of development and students

Today's students are tomorrow's alumni. That's why they should be knowledgeable about the rewards of philanthropy and the importance of fund raising at independent schools. The director of development's relationship with students is more direct and frequent if he or she teaches or coaches or advises. However, if the director of development is not a member of the faculty, other opportunities for close contact with students should be found.

10. The director of development and parents

The director of development and the head of school sat in the office of the chief program officer at the area's largest foundation. "Tell me about last year's annual fund campaign. Did you have 100 percent support from the trustees?" "Of course," replied the head of school. "And we had 100 percent support from parents as well." The foundation officer was impressed. "That really gives me something to talk about," he replied. Development directors who maintain a close relationship with the parents' association are best able to attract generous parental support. They keep parents informed about the costs of an independent school education, the increasing number of families who need financial aid, and the challenges of teaching first-generation independent school families about philanthropy. These directors of development understand that parent suggestions and parent fund-raising volunteers can enhance the success and professionalism of the development program.

11. The director of development and the school's attorney

The director of development needs direct access to legal advice. Most often, the head of school and the chair of the board's development committee keep the director of development informed. However, there are occasions when the director of development requires specific clarification about new or pending state or federal legislation related to fund raising, tax laws and charitable giving, tax-exempt bonds, conflict of interest, accounting regulations, and a host of other legal issues pertinent to a development program. It is too late when the school has been sued or the media jump on a juicy story.

12. The director of development and professional colleagues

Here are testimonials from directors of development about the rewards of communication with colleagues.

- "Of course my school is in competition with the area's other independent schools, but I never hesitate to call one of my counterparts for advice. And it's no mystery why we development directors in this area meet monthly. We are each other's strongest professional support."

- "Every time I attend [a] CASE or NAIS conference, I return charged up with new ideas, new challenges, new insights — and new contacts."

- "My career goal is to be a director of advancement at a college or university. My school head understands this, so I am encouraged to attend higher education association meetings. What a support system and contacts for the future!"

Other development directors understand both the opportunities and challenges of the job. They are best able to offer encouragement, understanding, counsel, and support.

13. The director of development and family and friends

The demands of development work and the pressures on a development officer are so great that there must be a conscious effort to provide balance in life. The director of development who understands the importance of family dinners, who calls home every day when he or she is on the road, who has season tickets to the symphony, and who works out each day in the school's fitness room is less likely to burn out and more likely to succeed on the job. All busy professionals should carve out time for a full life beyond their office door.

One of the great strengths of independent schools is the strong and persuasive conviction that all adults are colleagues and that, competition and rivalry aside, they have something significant to learn from each other. When these 13 key relationships are strong, all adults in the community can fulfill the school's mission, and they can model the respect and understanding they ask of the students in their care.

CHAPTER 11

Understanding Multicultural Constituencies

By Jane Heimerdinger

I n the 21st century, schools are working with increasingly diverse populations that bring a wide variety of ethnic, cultural, religious, and historical backgrounds to the community.

It is gratifying to see the many ways in which diverse and multiethnic groups are enriching the independent school world. Increasingly, multicultural populations are present, not only in the classrooms but also throughout the administration and staff.

Multicultural school campuses offer both a challenge and an opportunity for today's development professionals. Successful fund raising must blend established giving methods with the cultures and traditions of the school's diverse families. The development director must do the following:

- Look for new ways to engage all families in the school's social, education, volunteer, and philanthropic programs.

- Design a cultivation, solicitation, stewardship, and community relations program that appeals to varying cultures and recognizes and appreciates their differences.

- Make sure that the school's mission statements, brochures, magazines, newsletters, events, and calendars are culturally sensitive and are appropriate for, and understandable by, all members of the multicultural community.

- Help the teachers and staff acknowledge and reflect the diversity of the school's families in its educational program, library books, activities, and exhibits.

LEADERSHIP AND CHANGE

A development office team should be an instrument of leadership and change on the campus. If the development staff is to successfully market the school's need for charitable support of its academic programs, financial aid budget, faculty, and facility enhancements, it must embrace and educate others about the need for cultural sensitivity and the impact of diversity. In order to achieve the school's fund-raising potential, the development team members must be globally aware and have an understanding of and passion for differences in their communities and in the world beyond. Often, this is best done by development staffs that are themselves multicultural, reflecting the diversity of the wider community.

Cultural awareness and acceptance should begin with an annual review of newly admitted students with the admissions director in order to identify the diversity within families. Last names do not always tell the story. German households may have Korean children; Hispanic families may have African American children; Caucasian families may have Chinese children.

In addition, the members of the development staff should visit classrooms, talk to teachers, and participate in numerous school activities so that they can become aware of and sensitive to cultural differences. Staff members might serve as advisors to a Spanish Club, a Japanese Club, or an Arab American Club. They also might recruit appropriate parents to join them as advisors and partners at club events.

An annual September "Welcome Reception" at the home of the head of school can provide an opportunity for new families to meet school administrators, teachers, and other new parents. The development team should be present to get to know the new parents, to facilitate introductions, and to make sure the event runs smoothly.

HOW, WHEN, AND WHOM TO ASK

One of the first challenges is *how* and *when* to ask for a gift. Here generalizations can be dangerous; each group must be analyzed individually.

It is important to recognize the fact that, for many nationalities, philanthropy is a foreign concept. Therefore, education must precede the gift request. Multicultural families may not view their children's school as a charitable institution. More typically, they may feel that they have a business relationship with the school, from which they are purchasing a service at its market value. Therefore, the first step is to educate these families about (1) the importance of the nonprofit sector in the United States, (2) the role that it plays in promoting choice, innovation, and excellence, and (3) its dependence on voluntary support to remain financially strong.

In many cultures, giving starts at home with the nuclear family, which may include many who are not listed in the school's database. Relatives (even those living in other countries) are often regarded as immediate family members, and their views are paramount in philanthropic decision-making. Non-blood kin may be important decision-makers who pay the tuition, make the gifts, and represent the family in all school-related matters.

Furthermore, in some cultures, certain events create the motive for a charitable donation. It is wise for the development office to be aware of these moments and to encourage gift giving. Birthdays of elders, religious holidays (many times unknown to development officers), visits from relatives and friends from the home country, the arrival of a new baby, a national holiday, and even a death are among the occasions that some may wish to acknowledge with a gift to the school.

Among a school's vast numbers of ethnic groups, which might include Japanese, Native American, Asian American, Chinese, Indian, Cuban, Korean, Latino, Bangladeshi, Mexican, Pakistani, Middle Eastern, and others, approaches to giving, wealth, solicitation, stewardship, recognition, representation, meetings, and networking can be as different as night and day. Carefully consider labels, words, messages, and designations that distinguish groups. On the one hand, it is important to vary fund-raising materials and initiatives so that they are culturally appropriate. On the other hand, a school's fund-raising efforts should not be so varied and diverse that they send a mixed message or cause confusion within the community.

THE APPROPRIATE MESSAGE

When a school is asking for gifts, it is important to know the language, culture, and local community from which a family comes. A family from Kenya is quite different from a family from Nigeria; a Vietnamese family is different from a Korean family; a Samoan family is different from a Hawaiian. A particular group identification ("Hispanic," for example) may include people from a variety of countries and cultures.

Trust, shared values, and acceptance must be built over time. Schools must remember that in many cultures, family, including extended family, comes first. This includes a broad "cultural family" as well.

The importance of supporting a country of origin and a family's roots through membership in clubs and organizations can be strong. Often, this relationship is passed down from one generation to the next. Students in the school community may go together to day care, language immersion classes, cultural events, cooking classes, and social clubs that represent their common heritage. The school should acknowledge and respect these associations and join in celebration of events such as Cinco de Mayo (Mexico), Islamic New Year, Epiphany, Greek Independence Day, Boy's Day (Japan), and others.

Many ethnically diverse families may send a part of their earnings to relatives or neighbors outside the United States. This type of giving can be expected and ongoing. Showing respect, interest, and appreciation for families who support non-U.S. family members can help build closer relationships. Even though distance separates some families, their relationships may be just as close as those of families with grandparents and aunts and uncles living in the same neighborhood.

CULTURAL DIFFERENCES

Close long-term relationships, the hallmark of successful fund raising, must be appropriate and built over time. Here, awareness of cultural differences is essential. Matching a solicitor and a donor from the same nationality and providing ample cultivation before the gift request are often key to success.

In many Asian groups, giving is a family matter. The whole family may gather, but the elders lead the conversations and decisions. Such gatherings may involve the children. At meals and gatherings, the eldest sits at the head of the table with the most important family members on either side. It may be easier to discuss a gift in such a culture if the solicitor is an important member of the same ethnic group. Quiet reserve and a sense of dignity are expected.

Native Americans often prefer to hand-deliver a gift, presenting it directly to a school leader.

Pacific Islanders focus on serving the greater good. Because history and geography isolated the residents of these islands (Samoan, Micronesian, Hawaiian, and others), it was common practice to "share the wealth." Upon returning from a fishing trip, the fishermen would divide the catch evenly among the village's families. Even today, care of the *aina* (land) and the *Ohana* (many family members) is a priority. Pacific Islanders are happy to volunteer their time. This form of giving is of highest value and may replace monetary support.

SENSITIVITY TIPS

To be sensitive and appropriate, the staff should:

- Review messages and verbiage in written communications. Words are immensely powerful tools, and a catchy word, clever phrase, or misspelled word may have an offensive meaning in some cultures. While written pieces should be unique and innovative, they must also be culturally aware.

- Move beyond preconceived characteristics. A stereotypical assumption does not reflect deep thinking, understanding, and sincere respect for individuals. Stereotypical attitudes can be harmful, resulting in misunderstandings and unhappy constituents. It is important to remember that family composition, likes and dislikes, behaviors, preferences, experiences, and exposure are varied and different within ethnic groups.

- Create multiple messages and initiatives. While it is easier to produce one fund-raising flyer or to host a traditional annual event, it is more important to appreciate differences. Consider letters, mailings, and events that express understanding and acceptance of multiethnic families.

- Demonstrate the value of inclusiveness. Ignorance of cultural differences can be reflected in inadequate or inappropriate food choices or the scheduling of school events on holidays. However unintentional, these insensitivities create an impression of disrespect or a lack of inclusiveness.

- Balance responsibilities. The work of the development office must be balanced and productive. At the same time, development professionals should take the opportunity to participate in schoolwide activities in order to enjoy and to learn from the diverse community and to appreciate its richness.

SUBTLE DISTINCTIONS

It is important for school administrators and teachers to be aware of ethnic and cultural behavioral differences, which can be subtle.

Appropriate greetings may range from hugging, which is common in the Pacific Island population, to kissing on both cheeks as some Europeans do, to bowing as Japanese do. Generally, Asian groups do not have physical contact on meeting.

Eye contact protocols also vary. When engaged in conversation, Japanese nationals often do not have direct eye contact; Caucasian and Chinese encourage full eye contact; and Hispanics combine eye contact with touching on the arm or shoulder. In some cultures, an individual may stoop or bend in order to appear to be on a lower level than the person with whom he or she is conversing.

Fund-raising and communication messages and materials should always reflect a school's mission, style, and culture. However, be sensitive to the use of color. Particular colors can be significant. For example, in Chinese communities, white can indicate death; yellow signifies the *ying* and *yang*; and red means prosperity and luck. Pacific Islanders often use black, greens, and browns to reflect the land. Japanese combine red and white to represent happiness; for Native Americans, turquoise symbolizes giving and sharing.

The sensitive selection of photo images is also important. The same iconic images that convey feelings of friendship and security for some may appear offensive to others. Among different cultural groups, chrysanthemums

mean good luck, cherry blossoms are reminders of new beginnings, lotus
blossoms convey serenity, and bamboo symbolizes prosperity while a plume-
ria represents friendliness and acceptance.

CONCLUSION

Multicultural communities are giving communities. Differing cultures, life-
styles, interests, family dynamics, and responsibilities to the country of origin
all affect giving. Clearly, a multicultural community enriches the education
of all. However, one-size-fits-all fund raising is no longer an option. A development program must be appropriate and sensitive if it is to be successful.

CHAPTER 12

Partnering with Volunteers

By Ingrid Healy

Volunteers are the backbone of institutional success — whether they serve as coaches, members of the parents' association, annual fund callers, trustees, or in multiple other roles. But do school administrators really believe this? For example:

- Do the board, administration, and other school administrators appreciate how important volunteers are to fulfilling the mission and achieving institutional success?

- Has the school articulated its need for and support of volunteers in writing, perhaps in the handbook or strategic plan?

- Are volunteers asked for their input when new development programs are being considered?

- Does the school provide its volunteers with appropriate resources and space?

- Does the school periodically evaluate the volunteer experience and identify areas that need improvement?

If the answer to these questions is "no," it is time to upgrade the volunteer program, particularly if the school wants the volunteers to stay. Here is a countdown of the top 10 misconceptions in volunteer management that may actually alienate volunteers, as well as 10 tips that will make the volunteer experience successful.

10. Warm Bodies Are All the School Needs

Those who believe that "warm bodies" are all a school needs do not recognize the diversity of roles volunteers can fill or the diversity of skills they can offer.

Don't come up with tasks or busy work in order to get people interested and involved. Volunteers should believe they are making a real contribution. They should understand that their efforts are key to the success of a specific program or project.

> **TIP: Identify Real Opportunities for Involvement**
>
> Set SMART goals for each volunteer role. This will help identify volunteers who have the right skills and experiences for the job.
>
> Ask:
>
> **S**pecific –   Is the project well described and is its goal clear?
> **M**easurable –   How will achievement of the goal be measured?
> **A**ttainable –   Is the goal attainable?
> **R**ealistic –   Is it reasonable to ask a volunteer to do this job?
> **T**imely –   Is there a clear timeframe for the project?

9. Make It All About the School

It's not just about meeting the school's needs. It's also about the volunteer's desire to make a contribution that is useful, productive, and satisfying. Identifying and creating volunteer opportunities that match an individual's motivation, skills, and commitment with the institution's needs, challenges, and timeline provide experiences that are *mutually beneficial.*

Just as development officers understand the importance of "donor-centered fund raising," they must also understand that volunteer opportunities should be geared to volunteers' personal interests and motives. When an experience is fulfilling and rewarding, it is only natural to want to do it again.

TIP: Value Volunteers

Volunteer opportunities should not only support the goals of the institution, they should also provide an opportunity for volunteers to serve in a manner that is appropriate and meaningful *to them*. In identifying volunteer opportunities, ask:

- Is the volunteer assignment practical and will it be rewarding?
- Is it realistic to find volunteers to fill the role?
- Does the range of opportunities meet the different needs and interests of the available volunteers?

If the answer to these questions is "yes," the volunteer experience will be relevant and positive, and the best volunteer prospects will want to be involved.

8. Just Wing It!

When it comes to recruiting volunteers, winging it does not work. If a volunteer is recruited without a clear understanding and agreement about what the job will entail, surprises are likely to come early and often.

Volunteers may not be paid staff, but they need to be treated in a professional manner. Identifying *where* and *when* the school can use volunteers and *who* might be suitable for the various positions is only the first step. It is also essential to define clearly *what* the volunteers are to do.

Consider the trustee who is influential in the school community but, it turns out, is "uncomfortable" with fund raising or "philosophically opposed" to asking for money. Or the capital campaign chair who knows everyone on campus but complains, after agreeing to serve, that there are "too many meetings" and then wants to have a kickoff party before the leadership phase begins.

Has the director of development ever recruited a volunteer without providing a full explanation of the job because of fears that, with a full understanding of the job, the volunteer will not agree to serve? These scenarios may sound far-fetched, but, in fact, they do occur.

TIP: Create Clear Assignments

A volunteer job description can be an effective communications tool. It tells the potential volunteer what needs to be done. More importantly, it clearly describes the benefits to the volunteer. For example, in addition to helping the school achieve some important goals, the job might provide an opportunity to learn new skills or to meet new people.

Written volunteer job descriptions should include the following:

- Job title

- Purpose

- Tasks and responsibilities

- Time commitment and length of service

- Skills and qualifications

- Location of work

It's wise to consult volunteers when developing new job descriptions in order to ensure that the assignments not only meet the needs of the institution but also are interesting and attractive.

7. Beg, Plead, and Pray for a Few Stars

Recruiting volunteers is a balancing act. On the one hand, it is essential to reach beyond the inner circle of dependable current volunteers. To continue to call on previous volunteers may be easier, but it can also lead to burnout and to the appearance of being exclusive. Furthermore, having the same people — or the same small group of people — in the same positions may inadvertently give the impression that volunteers are members of an elite invitation-only club. On the other hand, casting the net too widely can be perceived as "anything goes" and can diminish the importance of the volunteer roles.

Once volunteer jobs are defined, target the ideal prospects carefully. A recruitment plan should include a process for responding to offers promptly so that no potential volunteer feels unappreciated or ignored.

TIP: Recruit Beyond the Inner Circle

- Host a volunteer fair at which parents, grandparents, and alumni can learn about different opportunities.

- Include information about different volunteer opportunities on the school's website.

- Create a volunteer application form that is available both online and at the school.

- Speak at school gatherings about available opportunities.

- And, of course, speak personally to the best prospects for a volunteer job.

Even if the initial job offered does not appeal, there may be other opportunities for those you would most like to be involved.

6. Remember, Ignorance Is Bliss

All volunteers need training whether they are new trustees, annual fund callers, or parents doing a two-hour shift at the school fair. For example, a new trustee should attend an orientation session about the board and its work. An annual fund caller needs to understand the fund-raising cycle, the case for support, and the preferred way to make calls. A parent helping at the school fair needs to know how to run the game or flip the burgers or take the money — whatever the task might be. Training should include a welcome, an overview of the job, and guidance on proper procedures.

To determine what kind of training is needed, identify the skills and knowledge volunteers will need in order to achieve success. In addition, ask current volunteers what training they wish they had had and what training they still need.

TIP: Provide Orientation and Training

Providing effective orientation and training helps volunteers understand their roles and how they fit into the whole enterprise. It ensures that they have the tools they need. During the training:

- Provide the history and background information about the program, project, or event, and describe its importance to achieving institutional goals.
- Outline relevant policies and procedures.
- Offer specific advice through role-playing.
- Highlight boundaries or limits of which volunteers should be aware.
- Because different people learn in different ways, reinforce the training session with a handbook or individual mentoring.
- Ask volunteers to evaluate their training.
- Be available to volunteer leaders. Encourage them to share concerns and questions. Touch base periodically to determine if they need additional resources.

5. Keep Them in the Dark

A mushroom thrives in the dark, but volunteers don't. Seek volunteer input and involvement. Include them in the planning process. And above all, share information.

When volunteers feel that they are not "in the know" or if they acquire information second-hand, they feel like outsiders.

Donors who talk about "we" rather than "I" and "you" clearly are engaged and invested. The same is true of volunteers. Comments like "I'm just a volunteer" or "What do they expect? It's not like they *pay* me to do this!" are warning bells. To avoid them, communicate regularly in order to keep volunteers informed.

TIP: Make Volunteers Feel That They Belong

Making volunteers feel like integral members of the team is an ongoing process. To create the sense of "we," remember the "I's":

- *Involve* them in program planning and evaluation activities.
- *Inform* them of relevant developments — in the school and in the programs with which they are involved.
- *Invite* them to regular meetings.

Efforts to make volunteers part of the "inner circle" convey the fact that you value them for their intelligent contributions as well as for their time.

4. Leave Them to Their Own Devices

Regular supervision and feedback are an essential form of volunteer support. For some people, "supervision" conjures up unpleasant thoughts of micromanagement or managing by constant direction. However, in effective volunteer management, supervision is really about building relationships. Ultimately, it is about setting up volunteers for success.

Communication should flow two ways. Provide oversight of volunteers and seek feedback from them. Ask how they are doing and what they require to succeed. Make sure that each volunteer has a staff member to whom he or she may turn for guidance and support.

TIP: Supervise through Ongoing Feedback

Supervise volunteers in a dynamic and ongoing fashion that encourages and facilitates two-way communication and invites ongoing discussion.

- Give guidance in a spirit of gratitude rather than as criticism.
- Provide positive reinforcement and identify opportunities for growth.
- Make specific suggestions.
- Be sure that volunteers understand the message. Watch body language for cues. Listen to individual comments and respond.

3. Ignore Comments and Complaints

Rather than wait for complaints, why not be proactive? Ask volunteers to evaluate their experience. Give them a way to provide feedback in a constructive manner.

Evaluations often seem negative. However, in truth, they can be a positive tool. Asking volunteers to evaluate their experience demonstrates that their role, their insight, and the quality of their work are valued. Creating an ongoing evaluation process identifies what is going well and what is not. Asking volunteers for their candid feedback on a regular basis enhances both the quality of the program and the quality of the volunteer experience.

TIP: Listen and Learn

Create an evaluation form that identifies both successes and opportunities to improve. Discuss individual responses with the volunteers. When receiving feedback:

- LISTEN. Be open to learning and to new ideas. Active listening involves restating what has been said to ensure that you have understood it correctly.

- Acknowledge the good intent of suggestions for change even if they are unrealistic. Be careful not to appear defensive.

2. It Should Be Treated Like a Job!

Volunteering is a leisure-time activity, so it is important to remember that volunteer jobs should be rewarding rather than feeling like work. Today's volunteers often have less free time to give; consequently, if they do not enjoy the experience, they are not likely to do it again.

In fact, volunteering can be a respite from "work" or other mundane activities and an outlet for energy and underutilized skills.

TIP: Make It Fun!

- Keep meetings of volunteers brief and efficient.

- Make it easy to participate by offering a variety of times and places to meet.

- Build in socializing and celebration. Provide lunch at noontime or snacks after work.

1. Thanks, but NO Thanks!

Stewardship shows donors that their gifts are appreciated and that they help the school fulfill its mission and achieve its goals in specific and meaning-ful ways. A volunteer's gift of time should be stewarded as well. Volunteer contributions should be appropriately recognized. The impact of their gifts should be highlighted. And just as stewardship of donors should be ongoing, so should the stewardship of volunteers.

TIP: Thank Them, Thank Them, and Then Thank Them Again!

Don't let volunteer efforts go unnoticed. Thanking volunteers should be both for-mal and informal through personal and spontaneous expressions of gratitude. Formal expressions tend to be public and predefined while informal expressions tend to be more personal and spontaneous.

Stewardship opportunities include the following:

- An annual volunteer reception or luncheon or breakfast
- Recognition in the annual report or magazine
- Awards and honors
- A personal thank-you note immediately following a job well done
- A surprise lunch or treat
- Verbal and unexpected praise

Following these tips will create a pleasant, supportive, and empowering en-vironment in which staff and volunteers partner together to achieve the school's goals. Volunteers will want to come back because they feel valued, informed, important, and respected. Most important, the volunteer experi-ence will be both rewarding and fun.

CHAPTER 13

Grandparents:
A Valuable Constituency

By Lucy E. Leitzell

According to a report from Grandparents.com and Focalyst, there are now over 70 million grandparents in the United States, making up "one of the largest and most powerful consumer segments." By 2025, one-quarter of the U.S. population will be grandparents.[1]

How can a school involve grandparents in its activities, inspire their loyalty, and gain their financial support? Grandparents can be significant independent school donors. Often they are willing and able to give to the school that is educating and nurturing their grandchildren.

Unlike parents of current students, grandparents may no longer be paying tuition at a college, university, or independent school. Unlike alumni, they are probably not raising a family, buying a home, or repaying education debts.

Many fund-raising strategies and tactics appropriate for other constituency groups, like parents of current students, apply to grandparents as well. For example, developing a successful grandparents program calls for a classic sequence of cultivation steps: identify, inform, interest, involve, and invest.

However, grandparents also present unique challenges and opportunities. A school that identifies and addresses those aspects creatively and con-

---

[1] Focalyst and Grandparents.com, "Meet the Grandparents: Introducing Today's First Time and Seasoned Grandparents," December 2007.

sistently will benefit from increased support and may also gain fresh insights into the core activities — such as communications and messaging, targeted events, and personalized approaches — that affect all constituencies.

ACCESS TO GRANDPARENTS

In schools with an established culture of philanthropy, it is usually not difficult to launch a grandparents program. In fact, in older schools, which many generations of a family have attended, some grandparents may be parents of alumni or alumni themselves. Their relationship is ready to ripen.

On the other hand, some schools that include constituencies new to independent school education may need to explain the reasons for involving grandparents in the school's program before current parents will consent to provide information about their own parents, who are at the center of this relationship nexus.

Parents may have concerns about an aging relative's interest in receiving information from one more "good cause." They may want to protect loved ones from appeals that could lead to approaches from other philanthropic suitors. They may need to screen invitations because the relative can no longer manage social interactions in a predictable way.

Schools that anticipate these legitimate concerns with a statement such as in the sample below have found that it establishes clear expectations and also serves as a guideline for the advancement program.

Sample

The Reynolds School is pleased to include grandparents and other friends and family members on its mailing list to receive the *Reynolds Report* (a quarterly magazine), the school calendar, and occasional invitations to plays and other special activities. Information about the annual fund is sent in October to everyone on the mailing list. If you would prefer that grandparents and other friends and family not receive requests for contributions, please inform the records manager in the Development Office (*records.dev@reynoldsschool.edu*).

IDENTIFYING GRANDPARENTS

Each school will seek grandparent information in its own way, but it is important to request it every year so that it remains current.

As part of the process, every school should do the following:

- Ask parents to let the school share information about its mission, history, and events with their parents.

- Be sensitive to the wishes of families who decline to have solicitations sent to their parents and other family members (and be sure that the database is configured to honor those decisions).

- Use care in differentiating between the addresses provided for routine mailings and those given for specific invitations, such as to Grandparents' and Special Friends' Day. The school will earn credibility by using information only as promised.

- Remember, the school will have no access to most grandparents without the goodwill of the parents. Respect their wishes.

INFORMING AND INVOLVING GRANDPARENTS

For grandparents, as for any other external constituency, communication plans should begin with the school's mission, program, vision, and future plans.

Recognize and counter misperceptions that some grandparents may have. For example, they may assume from a school's name that it is a formal, traditional school when it actually has a more informal atmosphere. If the school is nonsectarian, say so. Reference the school's core principles and give concrete examples of how those values are lived every day.

Consider why grandparents might decide to become involved with the school. Are they motivated by a passion for education? Nostalgic about their own years as parents of schoolchildren? Eager to have a sense of their grandchild's daily life at school?

Characteristics of the school — its traditions, location, and structure — will drive plans to involve grandparents. What works well for a small suburban elementary school may not fit an inner-city high school.

The objective of a grandparents program is to help them identify with aspects of the school that are important to them and to their own families. A campus visit may achieve that purpose, but it may not always be possible. Be creative and resourceful!

In addition to a grandparent's name, address, relationship, and telephone number, The Reynolds School also requests e-mail addresses so grandparents can receive a new electronic newsletter sent only to grandparents, with pictures, articles, and links to the many exciting activities that the school's students — their grandchildren — take part in every day.

GRANDPARENTS' AND SPECIAL FRIENDS' DAY

A Grandparents' and Special Friends' Day can distill the essence of the special relationship independent schools develop with their families. For some families whose grandparents live far away, a visiting day may be the only opportunity children will have to share their school, teachers, and friends with a grandparent or special friend.

"Special Friends" are family friends and members of a student's extended family who are important to a student, sometimes in a quasi-grandparent role, such as aunts, uncles, godparents, neighbors, and nannies.

As special events for grandparents are planned, remember to create realistic schedules and to build in adequate "passing time." Print programs in large type and amplify speakers' voices. Identify and eliminate trip and fall hazards. Arrange for reserved parking. Some schools take the additional precaution of requesting that the local emergency squad be onsite throughout the day.

FIND THE EXPERTS

Grandparents who have watched their own grandchildren thrive at a school may be able to identify other grandparents who have ties to the school or have a particular interest in supporting education. Ask for their advice:

- How and when should the case for grandparent support of the annual fund be presented?

- Should gifts from grandparents be counted and reported separately?

- Would a special project attract more enthusiastic support than a general annual fund appeal?

- How and why should the approach to grandparents be different from the one for parents of current students, alumni, or former trustees?

SAMPLE
Grandparents' and Special Friends' Day Letter

*At The Reynolds School, this letter is sent to every
school family in mid-January.*

Dear Reynolds School Parents,

In a few months, it will be our pleasure to welcome your child's grandparents and special friends to The Reynolds School!

Grandparents' and Special Friends' Day is a treasured annual RS event. The children and their teachers truly look forward to offering these important visitors a glimpse of a day at school.

Invitations will be mailed on April 16, using a collage of flowers created by the children and composed by our art specialist, Jane Smith. The invitations will include the following schedule of activities:

Grandparents' and Special Friends' Day, Friday, May 20
8:30 a.m. to 8:50 a.m.	Assembly
9:00 a.m. to 10:45 a.m.	Classroom Visits
11:00 a.m. to 11:45 a.m.	Reception

You should also feel free to extend an invitation to grandparents and special friends to attend the Spring Arts Evening on Thursday, May 19.

Each classroom teacher will develop a special activity for the children and their guests. More details will be sent home with your child closer to the date.

Parent volunteers will be on hand to direct guests. Please contact the main office if you would like to learn about volunteer opportunities, including helping with mailings.

The most important part of our planning is to be sure that invitations are sent to the grandparents and special friends that you and your child wish to invite. Please complete the enclosed form and return it to [the administrative assistant] before April 4. Note that we do not retain Grandparents' and Special Friends' Day address information from year to year, so we ask you to complete the form even if you provided this information in previous years.

Please do not hesitate to contact the school if you have any questions about these plans. Many thanks for your role in continuing this Reynolds School tradition.

Warmly,
John Smith
Head of School

Once there is a framework for a grandparents program, enlarge the advisory circle of grandparents into a committee. Recruit grandparents to be volunteers for specific projects, like the annual fund and the school's version of Visiting Day. These experts will help convince other grandparents to make the school one of their top philanthropic priorities.

Many grandparents are sympathetic to the need for funds to improve faculty compensation or to increase student financial aid. However, recognize that it may take more than a single school year to move a grandparent from an interested observer to a supporter of the annual fund, a major or capital campaign donor, or a candidate for a planned gift.

AN ANNUAL FUND CHAIR FOR GRANDPARENTS

Select an annual fund chair for grandparents from the group that is already providing advice.

The ideal candidate will have the potential to give more than a token amount. His or her leadership will be important. Look for someone who has had experience as a volunteer fund raiser. Most of all, choose someone who is accessible. Don't hesitate to ask a lot of questions. Asking for advice is splendid cultivation.

Honor the importance of this assignment with a seat on the board's development committee. Seek and respect his or her insights, connections, and validation.

TARGET THE APPEAL

Now the school has a special mailing list, a strong advisory committee, and a focused case for grandparents.

A committee of annual fund volunteers can do much more than stuff envelopes. The school will be able to send very personal appeals to other grandparents if the committee is selected carefully. Seek the widest possible distribution, both geographic and in relation to the age of their grandchildren. Have committee members review lists and sign letters to other grandparents whom they know or who live in the same area or have grandchildren in the same grade. Ask about the timing of approaches to grandparents they know well.

SAMPLE
Annual Fund Letter

Dear Andy and Sue,

You and I share an important bond: Our grandchildren attend The Reynolds School!

I delight in sharing my granddaughter Hallie's daily discoveries — whether it is her observation that Impressionism is her favorite style in art or her daydreams about following in the footsteps of her heroine, astronaut Bonnie Dunbar.

At the age of six, Hallie believes that there is nothing she can't do. A good school will reinforce her self-confidence, but a great school, like The Reynolds School, will give her the tools she needs to prepare the way to achieve her dreams.

Your contribution to the annual fund is key to sustaining the qualities that are hallmarks of a Reynolds School education — fine teachers, strong programs, and a warm and caring community. Every gift is important, because the tuition charged covers only about 80 percent of the cost of educating each child. No gift is too large or too small.

By supporting the annual fund, you not only enable The Reynolds School to meet its annual operating budget but also show your support for the wonderful faculty and staff who excite and inspire students like Hallie and your grandson Bobby every day.

Thanks to The Reynolds School, our grandchildren's future is bright! Please help support their education by participating in the annual fund.

Sincerely,

Donald Smith
Chair, Grandparents' Annual Fund Committee

Segment the group of grandparents as much as possible. Send a warm and welcoming letter to grandparents who are new to the school. Ask a senior faculty member to suggest a meaningful anecdote for grandparents who are themselves graduates or parents of graduates of the school. Thank donors for their generosity. Ask previous donors to give again.

UNDERSTAND THE CULTURE

Be aware that some grandparents may belong to a more traditional social culture.

These grandparents may have different expectations than parents of current students regarding forms of address, thank-you notes, and the protocol of who should sign which letter to whom. Err on the conservative side (use titles, not nicknames) until the relationship with a grandparent is clearly on a first-name basis. Consult the head of school and advisory group, establish a standard, and use it.

Just as it would in supporting a student, a school must always care about the individual and seek to nurture a genuinely respectful relationship with every one of its constituents. Always strive to write solicitation and thank-you letters that are specific to a particular donor. Record the names and nicknames of the children with other information about grandparents. If a child's name is Gordon but everyone calls him Billy, warm notes to his grandmother should refer to him as Billy, too.

AVOID PITFALLS

"How dare you!" exclaimed Mrs. Crown, the second wife of a man who inherited great wealth, speaking to a member of The Reynolds School's development staff. His son and daughter-in-law had just enrolled their four-year-old in The Reynolds School's excellent preschool. A week before the first day of school, Mrs. Crown and her husband were invited to a reception for other grandparents to learn about the school's capital campaign. She was astounded that the child's parents had not yet heard about the campaign to which she and her philanthropic husband had already been invited to contribute.

Mrs. Crown's remarks help explain the concerns some parents have about sharing grandparent information.

Development professionals must be prepared to counter overly enthusiastic volunteers (and sometimes professional fund-raising advisors) who are eager to jump to the older generation, especially if it includes people of wealth and philanthropic reputation, without engaging and working through the parents who are the link to these affluent grandparents.

It is almost always in the school's best interest to cultivate a long-term relationship with a family, rather than to secure an early gift that irritates the donor and sours future possibilities.

The school should endeavor to educate everyone about its fund-raising programs and policies in the following ways:

- Inform the entire community about purposes for which money is raised.

- Tell donors how their gifts are used.

- Educate the board and fund-raising volunteers about school policies regarding release of information (address, giving history).

- Educate professional advisors about the differences between an independent school and other nonprofits.

DON'T JUST ASK FOR MONEY

If it is to grow and thrive, a grandparents program should encompass more than predictable fund-raising appeals. Find opportunities for grandparents to see the school in action in non-fund-raising contexts. Do not assume that every invitation must require partnering with the grandchildren!

- Send those who live nearby invitations to campus events — plays, sports, book fairs, art shows, lectures, open rehearsals, concerts.

- Enlist annual fund committee members as special hosts to welcome grandparents on occasions when families arrive en masse.

- Design activities tailored to the grandparent generation's taste, pace, and availability.

- Consider events reflecting a special interest (a coffee reception on the morning of the book fair) or occasion (a reception for grandparents in another city to meet the visiting head of school).

- Distribute a calendar of events at which grandparents would be welcome.

Take full advantage of campus visits. Snap photographs for use in publications and fund-raising materials and to send to families as mementos. Offer tours to show how contributions have been spent and to point out present and future needs. Above all, feature the finest teachers doing what they do best.

GRANDPARENTS AS A RESOURCE

The extended community of grandparents and special friends can also lend its professional expertise to the school's program by offering occasional classroom presentations or formal lectures to which the community is invited or by providing internships for older students.

Does the grandparent community include authors, poets, or publishers? They might help the school invite an author to visit or start a writer-in-residence program. A medical researcher might present a lecture offering insights about the contributions of biochemistry to innovative therapies for chronic diseases. Some schools have presented programs by a grandparent for other grandparents on topics related to financial management, international travel, and upcoming cultural events.

FAMILY TREE

There are other reasons for getting to know grandparents.

A grandparents program fits nicely into a major donor research effort. The development staff may discover families who have inherited wealth, have their own foundations, or are linked to major charitable foundations or national corporations.

Be alert to indications of wealth and do additional research in order to support a formal proposal, perhaps directly to the individuals or to a foundation with which they are affiliated.

Be prepared for direct and unanticipated approaches from philanthropic grandparents. Develop a list of projects that could be funded, ranging from big dreams to furnishings and other more modest items. Review existing policies, or prepare them if they are not already in place, regarding gifts for endowment and for restricted purposes and planned giving vehicles.

BENEFITING FAMILIES

Particularly in communities where many families are transplanted from elsewhere, children may not have many opportunities to develop relationships with their grandparents. Relocations, divorce, single parents, and blended families require more effort from schools in helping children forge closer ties to their grandparents. Informing grandparents about the school and involving them in its advancement helps them bridge that gap.

Always present the grandparents program as a service to families, for that is what it is.

THE
SKILLS

CHAPTER 14

Marketing Communications: All About Branding

By Carol Cheney

More than 20 years ago, NAIS began publishing marketing handbooks for independent schools. Thumbing through those pages today, one is struck by how much has changed and how much has stayed the same.

The independent education scene has speeded up incredibly since the mid-1980s. In addition to the significant and comprehensive changes discussed in Chapter 1, technology is now playing an increasingly major role, not only in teaching and learning but also in communications.

Designers once thought the fax machine was the best thing since sliced bread until desktop publishing opened up the world of graphic design to anyone with a computer and a page layout program. Then along came digital cameras and printing and the Internet. In just a few decades, the world has been forever changed (and is still changing) by a stunning electronic revolution. Because there is growing consumer access to information technology in forms ranging from mobile telephones to podcasts, the audience is now in charge.

What has stayed the same? Some schools still chafe at the notion of selling and promotion. They often fail to understand that true marketing is a systematic approach to developing and maintaining mutually beneficial relationships between parties who have something of value to exchange with one another.

Marketing, incorrectly understood as a synonym for advertising, is seen as the equivalent of bad manners, which is one reason schools do not try to do a better job of differentiating themselves from competitors. Too often, schools are hesitant about initiating communications campaigns for fear of appearing needy. Trustees begrudgingly view resource allocation to marketing communications as an expense rather than as an investment that will yield important returns.

There continues to be a harmful disconnect between school strategic planning and business modeling on the one hand and purposeful communication with important audiences on the other. Many schools have no dedicated staff member to oversee communications and inadequate resources for keeping school audiences engaged and bringing new audiences into the fold. Schools are not always sure where to place the vast new responsibilities for web development and maintenance, and the use of e-mail is uncontrolled and unstoppable. As a result, these institutions expose themselves to the outside in an uncoordinated and haphazard fashion through academic, advancement, admissions, and other offices.

Schools that do support communications offices frequently do not enable effectiveness because they view the work of these shops as production-oriented — tactical rather than strategic. Communications staff often report to the development office, which naturally tips their allegiance and workload toward alumni and parent relations and fund raising. Many communications directors have no control over their budgets and no regular access to the senior administration.

Meanwhile, school boards and heads are dazzled by the promise of branding as a cure-all for finding new students, maintaining ties with alumni, and charming the neighbors. A clever logo and tagline, a set of focused messages distilling school mission, will solve all those doubts about self-identity and propel the school to popularity. What is often missing is the understanding that, while branding can and should be managed by the school, the way an institution is viewed and experienced by its audiences is really what a brand is all about. Branding begins with a marketing communications plan.

MARKETING
Definition of a Discipline

The term "marketing" refers to the intentional management of relationships for the mutual good of those engaged in them. Fundamental to successful relationship management are the following:

- Understanding the needs and expectations of important audiences

- Delivering on the promise of programs that remain true to the school's mission and are deemed valuable by its "customers"

- Creating an infrastructure to support an ongoing cycle of market research, planning, program implementation, and evaluation

THE MEANING OF MARKETING

As schools work toward an enhanced and strategic communications program, it is important for them to make the distinction between integrated marketing and sales/promotion, which carries a much narrower definition. Marketing embraces a broad perspective and centers on building and maintaining lasting relationships that have satisfying outcomes for all involved.

This definition of marketing applies both to commerce and to the nonprofit world, although the emphases are different, and schools can learn from Madison Avenue. Business is consumer-driven and bottom-line oriented. Companies change or develop products to meet the needs and expectations of buyers. They pay close attention to emerging, or nontraditional, audience segments whose buying power previously may have gone unrecognized, for instance, "tweenagers," Hispanics, and "gray panthers."

The advertiser's role is to help companies read the public's mind, not only to maintain market share against the competition for existing products but also to move out ahead — creating trends or "needs" with economic potential. The many brands of bottled and enhanced water, low-carb diet products, iPods, and Webkins are good examples. Corporate promoters study potential customers and work to stimulate a desire and build affinity for their product or services. The most effective advertising focuses on persuasion —

emotion, motivation, and promise — intangible aspects that will make the seller's product highly attractive to the targeted prospective buyer.

Corporate communications strategies aim at managing public perception of the seller's particular style or mystique, and this becomes an integral part of the creative approach. How does the public view the whole company? How is one company's mission or culture distinguished from another? Consider Starbucks and Dunkin' Donuts as examples. What is the brand and who are the faithful?

While businesses are market-driven and to some degree mission-sensitive, schools are mission-driven and market-sensitive. Profitability — the bottom line — is not the primary indicator of success. The values, tradition, and goals of the school do not yield to the whim of the public. To be successful, a school must engage in a dynamic adjustment of program and pricing that balances long-term interests with the expectations and needs of its audiences. Wireless campuses, faculty day care, directors of multiculturalism, expanded community service, club offerings, and Chinese instruction — these enhancements have all sprung from and are congruent with the core educational mission.

Meanwhile, a school's "total product" includes both generic and distinctive attributes that must be communicated clearly to various segments of its target audiences. Very often, schools speak "at" the people they want to influence with little regard for what those people want to hear, when they want to listen, and by what means they prefer to have their information delivered. At the center of institutional branding and identity should be a school's audiences (external focus), rather than a preoccupation with products and services (internal focus).

Schools build consensus — universally shared agreement about the mission, culture, and values of the school — by acknowledging and coping with the differences that exist in a complex organization serving a range of young people. This is especially important today when departments and programs within a school are competing for limited resources. Without consensus, schools will not be able to communicate in one voice to the constituencies they seek to influence.

INSTITUTIONAL BRAND: IDENTITY AND IMAGE

A school's identity must be so entrenched and so evident that it becomes the wellspring and promise of all its services, behavior, and actions.

All institutions must have a clear mission that is internally understood and embraced. Understanding and believing in the mission lead to a strong sense of belonging; organizational purpose and belonging are the fundamental aspects that make up identity. Schools are in a service business; their intangible assets are inseparable from the people who deliver them. How a school relates to everybody with whom it comes into contact is a vital aspect of identity. The services a school performs must project its standards and values. The configuration and state of a school's facilities and campus are compelling manifestations of identity. The communications vehicles must have a consistent quality and character that accurately and honestly reflect the whole institution.

It is important to understand that a school's brand is at the intersection between what its customers value and the institution's unique strengths. Perception of the school's essence is created by a constellation of impressions, including direct experience with the school, word of mouth, and person-to-person contacts. In order to manage their brand, independent schools must engage in a continuous cycle that begins with a promise that resonates with its audiences, continues with clear communication and delivery (or fulfillment) of that promise, and, as a result, creates meaningful and ongoing relationships with all constituencies. ("Do what I want better than anyone else, and I will love you forever.")

Very few institutions treat all their interactions as part of a seamless whole. (College counseling, grade reports, parent-teacher conferences, and the state of the locker rooms are just as much a part of image and brand management as the admissions open house and annual fund appeal.) If a school is not consistent in projecting its identity — sending out poorly executed, conflicting, or incomplete messages — it will foster incorrect perceptions and perpetuate out-of-date stereotypes. The old adage "If you don't tell your story, someone else will" could not be more true.

In the end, institutional identity is the responsibility not only of the school's advancement, admission, and communications staff or consultants but also of the people who run the institution. True marketing is more than just a sales campaign, logo, and slogan; it is a deep commitment to a particular way of doing and being.

WHAT IS POSITIONING?

The mission statement, while describing a school's core vision and beliefs, is often both generic and general, similar to the mission statements of many other independent schools and the implied missions of some public schools. Viewed from a marketing perspective, the mission statement fails to single out the true distinctive attributes and characters of individual institutions and instead offers important school audiences the lofty, futuristic language of an ideal.

The position of the school, defined within the competitive marketplace, must also be articulated and understood. It is at this point that many schools do not make the connection between what they believe about themselves and how they are perceived by important audiences. Position focuses on a school's differentiating attributes, setting it apart from the competition. According to marketer Ford Kanzler, "From a management perspective, positioning is the heartbeat of an effective communications plan. The positioning statement addresses seven essential questions:

- Who are you?
- What business are you in?
- What audience(s) do you serve?
- What is needed by the market you serve?
- Who is the competition?
- What is different about your business?
- What unique benefit is derived from your services?"[1]

Trustees and senior administrators, informed by appropriate market research, must answer these questions and then use the answers as the basis for school messaging.

---

[1] Ford Kanzler, "The Positioning Statement: Why To Have One Before You Start Communicating," online at *www.marketingprofs.com.*

Managing a school's brand means guiding the target audiences' perceptions of the school, emphasizing the positive while overriding inaccurate or negative impressions. It means not hiding your light under a bushel, but proactively building buzz. It is important to remember that reinforcing a school's position depends on communicating detail — simple, clear, substantiated claims, not fluff or platitudes.

THE ROLE OF RESEARCH IN COMMUNICATIONS PLANNING

Many schools do not probe beyond stereotypes they hold about their competitors or know what is happening in the educational marketplace to be able to draft a positioning statement. It requires the will to look from the outside in and to supplement anecdotes and opinions with hard data. It also requires questioning members of the school's extended family who may be only marginally engaged. It is almost more important to find out about their attitudes and ideas than to hear from "the choir" of key volunteers and top donors.

Schools are usually sitting on caches of useful information that, when aggregated and accessible, can be helpful in priming the research pump.

MANAGING SCHOOL IDENTITY

In working toward a more consciously managed institutional identity (brand management), schools must think about how their communications initiatives can help accomplish the following:

- Achieve coherence — present the institution as clear and comprehensible with its different services and programs relating to each other

- Create meaningful symbolism — represent core essence and attitudes, so that everyone who works for the school can share and communicate the same spirit

- Establish position — differentiate the school from its competitors in the marketplace

Industry information is available through NAIS and geographical/affinity group associations. Individual school input comes from all sorts of sources, including reaccreditation self-studies, reunion questionnaires, campaign feasibility studies, admission inquiries and telethon calls, informal discussions at events, and the grapevine. Schools are wise to survey their referral sources, college freshmen, teachers, families who leave the school voluntarily, and admitted students and parents. Others survey alumni about the relationships they wish to have with their alma mater, understanding that interests and needs will vary according to decade, gender, geography, and other factors.

More systematic conversations and focus groups provide important "qualitative" information (personal opinion) about satisfaction, communication preferences, evaluation of events, and even school personality. Such data, while usually drawn from a small fraction of the school's alumni or parent body, offer important insights into how a school is viewed (rightly or wrongly) and help design appropriate messages for different audience segments. Qualitative information has another important benefit: It informs senior administration about concerns requiring more systematic study using quantifiable online or telephone market research.

THE PSYCHOLOGY OF COMMUNICATING EFFECTIVELY

The overall communications goal is to bring people up-to-date, to expand their knowledge, and to build goodwill and pride. It is helpful to think about marketing communications as a continuum that motivates favorable behaviors ranging from awareness to sustained commitment among target audiences, including prospective families and teachers, current parents, and alumni.

Awareness
One has to know that an institution, service, or product exists in order to consider it. Mass media and direct mail advertising, physical presence, media relations, the web, and community involvement are effective communications tools that produce increased visibility and name recognition and stimulate positive word of mouth.

Information

Once aware of an institution that may be of interest, a prospect may want to seek information. Schools must present their services and programs in a way that piques the interest of prospective families and faculty, referral sources, and alumni and friends. A school's formalized communications vehicles, such as the website, suite of admission materials, magazine, and newsletters, all play important roles. Prospect lists and records management make it possible for schools to move targeted audiences into closer relationships with the school. Correspondence personalized through mail-merge programs is mandatory.

Evaluation

Individuals then begin to weigh the merits and value of an institution for them personally. The Reynolds School will be compared with other private schools and public schools. Its distinctive qualities must be communicated clearly and compellingly at a more personal level. On the fund-raising side, alumni and parents must be motivated by its case for support as they make decisions about the allocation of their charitable expenditures. The Reynolds School should make donor prospects feel like insiders.

Prospective families will view recruitment events and print and electronic communications as a reflection of the quality of the management and education that the school offers. Their questions must be anticipated.

Trial

Interested prospects put great store in the opinions of friends and advisors whom they respect. Current students are very important spokespeople, as are parents, referral sources, faculty, and alumni. In publications and on the website, testimonials about the school's quality, reputation, and ability to deliver on its promises help sway opinion and move a "sale" forward. Word of mouth is a powerful tool.

Because an independent school education is such a high-ticket purchase with difficult-to-quantify benefits and huge emotional ramifications, the right school becomes one of a family's most important and conspicuous choices. All potential donors and alumni in particular are being approached by their colleges, their children's schools, and other institutions. Their interest must also be courted and sustained through ongoing contact.

Adoption

After moving successfully through the first phases, the constituent will move to adoption, that is, take action (apply, donate money, volunteer, etc.). This is closing the deal, and it relies on personal attention as the most important communications tactic. What does a school do to make people feel that they have made the right decision? On the admissions front, the child is the direct consumer, but the parents pay the bill. Their needs and interests are overlapping but different — both must be attended to.

Reinforcement

Communication from the school must continue systematically to promote sustained adoption and, ultimately, advocacy. This long-term phase is what nurtures student retention (family satisfaction) as well as an ongoing close relationship with alumni, past parents, former faculty, and good will in the community. Systematic stewardship and recognition must become an important focus for communication on an ongoing basis.

The quality of student reports and parent meetings, coach and advisor interaction, new student orientation, and other informal and routine communications is part of the marketing mix that will sustain and increase enrollment. Annual stewardship letters to named endowment donors may stimulate additional or larger gifts. Faculty evaluation and recognition must be handled evenly, conscientiously, and deftly every year. Personal interactions have enormous power, well beyond even the most wonderful magazine or annual fund appeal.

Mixing the Media

When allocating precious budget and staff resources, remember that a mix of different communications vehicles works best in both friend and fund raising.

Mass media and general messages (website, advertising, publicity, viewbook, etc.) are generally most effective in the first two phases of the process (awareness and information), while the personal contact with friends and "sales representatives" (school official, trustee, parent, alumnus) is key during the evaluation, trial, and adoption phases.

Later, an appropriate mix is needed to justify the purchase decision and to maintain commitment. Communications tactics should be selected to move audiences through these stages, with the understanding that the expectations and needs of different individuals and constituencies will require different vehicles and interactions and that expectations and needs may change over time.

Specific goals and strategies (and most of a school communicator's energy) will focus on annual objectives in the area of student recruitment and retention, constituency relations, fund raising, and community relations. This work will be guided by strategic priorities established by the trustees and senior leadership. Messages and themes for the more formal communications will grow out of the positioning statement and should be the province of the director of communications.

MARKETING COMMUNICATIONS MANAGEMENT

Marketing communications is everyone's responsibility. As a philosophy, marketing establishes the way a school behaves toward those it serves and, as such, it involves the entire community.

Marketing happens during every interaction between a school and its audiences. The purpose of marketing communications is to manage relationships through carefully crafted messages and tactics.

Each year, schools produce dozens of publications, flyers, newsletters, reports, and ads; send out even more letters and e-mails; and add to the omnipresent website. These communications materials should be part of an integrated, intentional marketing effort to concentrate resources, establish a stronger "brand," and advance institutional goals. Because they have a significant impact on school reputation and image, these messages must be unified in their content, presentation, and timing.

Centralizing Oversight

At the forefront of this effort should be the communications office. Centralizing the communications function in one office at the school is key to a school's ability to do this work successfully.

Marketing practice has four major components:

- Research

- Planning

- Implementation

- Assessment

In the best scenarios, the director of communications is involved in institutional decision-making at the top level and administers an office that serves as the in-house creative agency for the institution's entire outreach program, supporting the needs of admission, development, alumni, and parent relations, as well as all other offices and departments that need help in developing and producing formal communications pieces.

In an independent office, the director of communications operates as a strategic thinker and planner, is a good collaborator, and is knowledgeable about online communications, publications, public relations, advertising, events, and community relations. The director is a skilled manager of staff and outsourced services. Small communications shops in particular need good writers.

Schools should not rely on volunteers to carry out the work of institutional communications since this presents an unrealistic picture of what it costs to integrate a marketing communications program into the annual budget. Further, because volunteers have different skill sets and limited time, there may be huge swings in productivity and quality using this "free" source of labor.

Photography

Documentation of special events that occur during the school year should also be handled by the communications office. Using the calendar as a guide, the director of communications should plan photography for the year, anticipating the needs of all major publications, website, posters, and displays. Photo subjects should include a full documentation of the daily life of the institution, not just special events.

Information Management and Printing

Schools benefit from examining the mailing lists generated by various offices in order to integrate their databases and to set policy guidelines regarding the retention of different categories of constituents in the computer systems.

A COMMUNICATIONS CALENDAR

The director of communications leads a work group that prepares a truly comprehensive annual master calendar that includes the following:

- Opening and closing dates, holidays, vacations, days off, exam periods, annual school celebrations, and meetings

- Web update schedule

- Mailing dates for invoices sent by the business office to parents

- On-campus special events or activities, including those initiated by individual offices (development, alumni, head of school, admissions, academics, college counseling, summer programs, etc.)

- Off-campus special events; travel by the school head, director of development, and director of admissions

- On-campus visitor dates, including visits by college representatives

- Mailing dates for invitations

- Mailing dates for appeals, reminders, stewardship letters

- Mailing/posting dates for magazine, newsletters, special publications, push e-mail, etc.

- Mailing dates for recruitment materials

- Mailing dates for information packets to current parents and volunteers

- Dates for publishing media and directory ads

- Timing of market research and other special communications projects

This calendar allows a school to see at a glance how often and when it is communicating with different audiences.

Eliminating duplicate entries and capturing and maintaining good contact data allow the school to more easily personalize correspondence and to take advantage of customizing communications to specific audience segments.

Whenever possible, schools should replace photocopiers with high-capacity laser printers that can receive files electronically from computers linked to them around campus. This technology can facilitate personalization and reduce unnecessary or redundant print pieces.

Budget

The director of communications should have responsibility for the magazine, publicity, and community relations budgets and joint responsibility for the website budget with the information and technology team. He or she should also work closely with admissions, advancement, and other departments as they prepare their individual budgets.

Schools should aggregate the costs of hardware and software, outsourced services, photography, production, media buys, materials, and printing, as well as website serving and maintenance, in order to get a complete picture of the magnitude of their annual budget in this area. The board and senior administrators should view these expenditures as an investment that reflects the importance a school places on marketing. Measurement of this investment cannot be reduced to an easy cause-and-effect equation, and significant results may not come immediately. However, undersourcing this critical component of school management or allowing mediocre work to represent the school will lead to a diminution of institutional stature and possibly the failure of school mission.

Going to the Next Step

Moving key constituencies from their current levels of engagement with a school requires a shift in philosophy about marketing and communications and a more strategic, creative, and persuasive sequence of initiatives. Greater cooperation among offices is essential to this effort, but, in the end, these changes will serve the school in a very positive way.

I owe a deep debt of gratitude to these experts, whose teachings have shaped my thinking: Robert Sevier, Stamats; Wally Olins, Saffron Brand Consultants; J.D. Rayburn, Florida State University; and Jeffery T. Wack, JTWack & Company.

CHAPTER 15

Making the Most of Technology

By Kevin J. McAllister

The one constant about technology is change. The challenge for an independent school and its development director is to evaluate which changes are important to adopt, which are cost-effective, which are a passing fad, and which, if ignored, will negatively affect the institution. Ignoring new technology can potentially be costly.

Technology is essential to the philanthropic process. Technology empowers its users, increasing productivity and extending the power of communication. The artful use of appropriate technology can help manage the following:

- Data storage and retrieval
- Communication
- Productivity
- Research

Philanthropy is undergoing a generational change. The seasoned, mature professionals now guiding many institutions learned their craft in a very different world. Their assumptions about how to communicate, how to budget, and how to plan events were created in a world of fax, phone, personally signed notes, and glossy quarterly magazines. Today, we have cell phones, e-mails, websites, Internet phones, webinars, podcasts, video sharing, multi-person chats, and social networks. Budgets, staffing, and planning must accommodate these changes.

How do you decide which technology tools to buy or what services to add? Since adding some of these technologies may take 18 to 24 months, how do you know that this latest "thing" will be relevant once it is finally rolled out? Is it worth investing $50,000 to $100,000 and hundreds of hours of staff time on something that may be a passing fad?

If there were directions and products that were clearly the best, planning would be simple. What is clear is that more people are using the web, and that these users expect more services such as online giving and online event registration. They are comfortable with and expect e-mail. Printed letters and magazines have become less desirable, less timely, and more expensive. Independent school constituents are going online for connecting and sharing, but they are overwhelmed by all the choices and services.

While no office can stay on top of or keep pace with every change, it is prudent to be aware of trends, leave room in budgets for new expenses, and shorten strategic time frames.

These are some of the questions to review often in strategic budgeting and planning for technology:

1. What mix of web vs. campus data systems will offer maximum productivity?

2. What is the role of the web in communication?

3. What are the roles and cost-effectiveness of print?

4. Which essential tools allow the office and staff to be organized in a real-time, anytime/anywhere world?

5. Which technologies do constituents consider commonplace and worthwhile?

6. To what extent should the development office be integrated with the school's overall technology?

This is not the time to rely on old habits — to the contrary, it is a time of growing possibilities. The opportunity to connect with constituents in real, personal ways across the nation and the world has never been greater. Trustees and administrators must act with prudence and wisdom, but they must also be knowledgeable about the new opportunities that technology offers.

In the 21st century, there is no such thing as a non-techie. Everyone can successfully integrate proven technology into his or her work.

COPING WITH CHANGE: GRADUAL EVOLUTION, QUANTUM LEAPS, THRESHOLDS, AND LIMITS

Educators have been wrestling with the integration of technology into teaching for the past 20 years. The technology tools that workers of the future will need are often not those used or taught in school. The schedule of the school year follows farming cycles from the last century. Much curriculum delivery is little changed from the days of slate and chalk. The curriculum is often dictated by the entrance requirements of colleges, which themselves resist change. Tools exist to transform educational practices, but traditional school leadership is often unprepared or unwilling to address the structural issues.

The development office faces the same tools vs. practices conundrum. It is often impossible to separate technology issues in a school development office from technology issues schoolwide. The networks, databases, and budgets are usually intermingled.

Gradual Evolution

In recent times, computing power has doubled every two years. This has proven true with many aspects of technology, including processor speed, hard drive storage size, and digital camera resolutions. As a result, new technology gets old very fast, and radically new possibilities become available often. The latest model computers that the development office just bought are already barely up-to-date by the time they are delivered. The solution is to buy less but to buy more often.

Misconception 1: The development office staff needs new computers because theirs are too slow.
Almost any computer less than three years old will support most needs of the common user — word processing, Internet searching, e-mail, chatting, spreadsheets, and the office database. Faster computers for staff members ed-

iting video or needing advanced graphics may be necessary, but again the need is far less than generally suggested. Even when the applications seem slow, the speed of the computer is often not the weakest link.

Usually, speed and storage increases alone will not impact productivity. A car that can accelerate faster or hold more gasoline is not going to radically change driving options or habits. A spell-check that replaces errors in a 16th of a second instead of an eighth is not going to affect writing productivity significantly. The same concept applies to buying new computers.

Misconception 2: Deleting files will make the computer faster.

People sometimes think that a full hard drive "slows" the computer in the same way that hiking with a heavy pack slows a hiker. The reality is that the hard drive is always full — storing zeros and ones. Switching some of the zeros to ones does not "fill" the hard drive. Deleting old files usually does not make the computer faster. If the files are scattered throughout the hard drive, indexing the directory can cause minor delays but generally not enough to be noticeable. Utilities that defragment the hard drive can help. However, the fundamental cause of slowness is most often elsewhere.

Misconception 3: A faster computer will make web searching faster.

If searching the web seems slow, the culprit may be the network, the school firewall, or the target website itself. A firewall acts like the security check at the airport. Each and every packet of information is stopped, inspected, and questioned before entering the school network — the more rigorous the questioning, the longer the delay. The IT department should balance performance and access with security, just as the airport staff does.

If many students or faculty members access the network at the same time, such as during lunch or at the end of the class day, performance speeds can drop significantly. Faster computers will not help. Only so many cars can travel the freeway before traffic jams occur. However, as with car traffic, there are ways to give certain users "priority lanes" on the network. The IT department should evaluate whether or not this is cost-effective or fair. Finally, if the target website is busy or slow, a faster computer will see the same delays.

A far more compelling test for deciding to buy new computers is whether or not the current machines can support newer operating systems and newer software. That should be the most important factor when a school is deciding on hardware upgrades.

Quantum Leaps

In contrast to the need for new computers, there are numerous ways in which new technologies can provide a quantum leap in performance or potential. These technologies are not just slightly faster or better, they are hundreds or thousands of times better. Often, they also offer new functionality.

E-mail makes it possible to correspond in seconds with constituents around the globe — something that would take weeks by letter. The web allows instant worldwide publishing of text, pictures, or video. Internet telephony provides free worldwide calling. Free teleconferencing services can replace expensive previous technologies. Easy teleconferencing can reduce the need for physical travel.

Misconception 4: Powerful software can take the place of training and expertise.

Seductive new technologies permit rank amateurs to do things heretofore only possible with sophisticated, expensive equipment, which was generally owned only by highly trained professionals. With a mid-priced camera, you can record a remarkably clear video with sound. This footage can be edited with impressive transitions and titling and "published" to the world for little cost. Anyone with patience and a few hours can create a video that would have cost tens of thousands of dollars 20 years ago. Being able to edit and add effects, however, does not ensure that you can produce a professional video.

The same is true for desktop publishing and graphics. The software allows adventurous beginners to produce remarkably advanced effects. The fact that someone can make letters of any size or font, color them, and place them at any angle on a page does not mean that he or she has graphic design skill or experience. A school would never allow a faculty member to build a dorm just because he or she can use a router and a skill saw. To produce professional quality publications — print or web — a school must rely on trained designers and editors, either on staff or by contract.

Regardless of the software, budgeting for training each year on a continuing basis is absolutely essential. In addition, the development staff must have access to adequate and timely tech support.

Threshold Differences

While technologies improve over time, there are also threshold breakthroughs that have significance beyond incremental advances. This is an important distinction. As new technologies emerge, certain new activities become possible. They are not generally useful, however, until three threshold barriers are crossed:

- The technologies are easily understood and used.

- Their time or cost is significantly less than the alternative.

- A sufficient number of people know about the technologies and are using them productively.

At some point, the technology becomes so commonplace that the only ones who are not affected are those who actively avoid it. People can refuse to watch TV, own a cell phone, or fly in planes, but, in general, it is acceptable to plan activities assuming that most of your constituents can access these technologies, which have passed the threshold.

Similarly, when some new tasks are too time-consuming to even bother, then, in effect, they are not possible. Buying inefficient technology will not increase productivity because no one will use it.

Threshold Examples for Philanthropy

1. E-mail

This technology has been around since the late 1970s, but it was not until the mid-1990s that it became a common form of communication. Until it became commonplace for professionals to receive e-mail, sending e-mail was not an effective means of communicating. However, today it is the rare professional, parent, student, or grandparent who does not have an e-mail account.

E-mail blasts. Now that e-mail use is common, sending e-mail to large groups of individuals is possible, effective, and accepted. The technologies for doing this vary greatly, however, and only some pass the threshold test for time. For example, a development director wants to send an e-mail to all the SYBUNTs or to every parent who gave more than $500 the previous year. Many website technologies support e-mail blasts. What the website may not support, however, is the sending of a blast to such a group based on a search of the data. Herein lies the threshold.

In Office One, the task consists of querying the database, exporting the resulting names, opening the website mailer, flagging the 100 to 500 names, and creating and sending the e-mail message. Querying the database is so complex that only one or two staff members are capable of the task. Transferring the results to the web is both complex and done so infrequently that it requires significant relearning and support each time. The overall process could occupy several hours to the better part of a day. During a busy period, the task might be delayed for several days or weeks.

In Office Two, the staff person or development director performs an easy find in the database, pulls up an e-mail screen within the database, then writes and sends the e-mail from the database. Personalized constituent data is merged directly into the message. The entire task is accomplished in 45 to 60 minutes.

Blast e-mail technology is effective in Office Two and will be used often. Office One will use it rarely, given the time threshold. Office One is at a competitive disadvantage, based mostly on the choice of database system and web services.

2. Built-in, customizable reporting vs. exported reporting

No matter what the size of the office, there is a need to summarize data to present at meetings of the staff or the board. The more easily such reports can be created, the more time can be saved.

In Office One, the database is queried by a single trained staff member and exported to a different software. These data are manipulated and edited and adjusted, and this process takes the better part of a day. Between the time of the export and the meeting, new gifts are entered into the system. Either the report must be redone or the development director must indicate that the data are not complete.

In Office Two, the reports are created directly in the database. The reports can be adjusted or duplicated without exporting data. Hours or minutes before the meeting, an accurate, up-to-the-minute report is run.

The willingness of the development director to experiment with new reports is vastly different in Office Two. Furthermore, the reports are timelier and more accurate, and they can be adjusted without discarding past work or redoing tasks. Office Two is much better able to adapt and to report accurately because of its choice of database systems.

Limits

Once a new technology is common, it may become either less innovative or less effective, just as traffic in large cities makes auto travel much less efficient.

E-mail is a now a common means of communication, but there are limits. Filters may block important e-mails by accident, and users switch e-mail accounts frequently. It's not safe to assume that a critical e-mail blast sent to 100 constituents actually reaches the intended recipients.

Recent Internet services make it possible to publish videos, podcasts, or pictures to the world for little to no cost. When only a few people used this technology, the postings were noticed. With thousands, even millions doing so, the postings may be ignored.

Misconception 5: If it is built, they will come.

People can receive only so many e-mails, belong to only so many communities, read only so many blogs, and watch only so many webinars. At what point does a school overload rather than cultivate its constituents?

Schools can create web communities and social networks for alumni, parents, and other community members. While this can be an effective way to connect groups of people, the prevalence of networks and communities makes it unrealistic to think that a significant number of alumni will visit the site regularly. More realistically, they will visit to research their reunion or to respond to a solicitation e-mail. This poses a dilemma. Is it better to provide a powerful medium that is scarcely used or to avoid the cost and upkeep and seek other means of connection? Would a simpler website area be used more frequently and hence be more cost-effective than yet another interactive community?

THE FUND-RAISING DATABASE

Data about constituents and their giving are one of the school's most valuable assets. Often, that information is stored in ways that do not invite effective use. A staff member enters data in order to generate periodic reports. Maintaining and using the data is a staff task. In some offices, the development director never logs into the system because he or she does not consider it a worthwhile use of time. The database is either too difficult to use or it does not provide sufficient value when it is used.

Times have changed. Searching and exploring and mining that data may be the key to developing new strategic directions. Being familiar with the data is the best way to ensure timely, meaningful contact with key constituents. Like the web, a cell phone, and a laptop, the database should be an essential tool used every day by every development director. Lack of knowledge can be expensive.

A database is a software application used to organize data into fields and view screens. There are any number of commercial products designed for philanthropy that come with predefined fields and screens. What is not apparent at first glance, however, is that the ability to use those data varies significantly from system to system. Search mechanisms, the database structure, automation functionality, integration capabilities, reporting capabilities, security options, and more will dictate how well the database allows the users to accomplish tasks effectively. The time threshold for common tasks may not be met.

Some schools create their own databases. Their intent is to save $20,000 to $80,000 by building a system rather than purchasing a commercial product. As they attempt to perform productivity tasks or to create complex reports, they quickly realize that something seems to be missing. A powerful, functional data system for an office is far more than fields and screens. Choosing a poorly functioning "free" database may be the most expensive decision a school can make.

Commercial products are not always more effective than homegrown solutions. Some systems are only designed for data entry and reporting and are single-user systems or are hard to modify or search. To meet the needs of a development office, the database should support four uses:

- Organization
- Productivity
- Noodling
- Reporting

Organization

In an organized office, there is a place for everything and everything is in its place. A database should provide the required fields for storing all the data used in development. It should also have a proper underlying relational structure to permit detailed searching and reporting.

Given that change is constant, if the database does not provide potential additional fields and additional ways to view the data, it is inevitable that, eventually, work will be done outside the system. At that point, the office will have at least two databases and, over time, perhaps several. A database system that is not flexible or does not allow for customization and extension will be costly to operate in terms of lost productivity.

Productivity

A primary reason for storing data about constituents is to facilitate communication with them, generally in the form of labels, letters, or e-mails. If productivity tasks can be accomplished only by exporting data, the value of the system is dramatically lowered.

Noodling

"Noodling" is informally sifting through the vast sandbox of data. Before more friendly databases became available, noodling was either impossible or extremely tedious. Today, given the right database system, it is much easier.

Too many development directors are ignorant of this powerful tool, either because their current database makes noodling impossible or because the learning curve is too steep. Usually, the development director is not expected to enter gifts, produce thank-you letters, or design reports. But the development director should be able to browse through his or her own database for nuggets of information.

For example, the development director should be noodling for the following information:

- Who came to a particular event last year and what gifts were linked to it?

- What large gifts did parents give last year?

- Which current parents have given more than $500 in a year?

- Which grandparents are major donors?

- Who were the biggest alumni donors during the past 10 years?

- What SYBUNTs will be coming to this week's event?

- What gifts have been made by new trustees this year?

- What gifts came from faculty during the past three years?

- How many attended the auction last year and how much money was raised?

- Who in the local area played soccer or had Mr. Jones as an advisor?

- What events did Ms. Donor attend last year and what is her giving history?

Noodling is different from reporting and even from data mining. Being able to educate yourself as a development director quickly and flexibly about key constituents is the greatest value that a school's data provide.

Reporting

Having the ability to aggregate data into totals and to present that data in lists and groups is the fundamental reason for storing data in databases.

In addition, some results of noodling might be useful as a report. Examples are a list of all parents who have given more than $500 in the current year or a list of constituents in Chicago, Atlanta, or San Francisco.

Rather than just listing the results of a query, true reports consolidate data and include totals, percentages, and sub-summaries. Some systems require exporting to produce reports or lists. Such a system will dramatically reduce the desire and ability to report. Reports must be available at the touch of a button and accurate to the moment to be useful. This is another threshold issue.

DATA INTEGRATION

The data needed by a development office fall into two main categories — the constituents to solicit and the gifts they make. For a new school, the development constituents may consist largely of current parents. In older institutions, alumni, past parents, grandparents, past grandparents, friends, and other constituents far outnumber current parents. In either case, it is important to keep accurate parent records.

A subset of that constituent data, such as biographical and address information of current parents and students, is also used by other offices. For example, accurate information about the current parents is needed by the registrar, admissions office, college guidance office, business office, and others. This leads to some key questions: How does the school keep current parent data accurate in all of these offices? If the database is shared, who is responsible for the standardization, coordination, and accuracy of the information? How is it communicated to those who need it? Does integrating biographical information for current parents across the campus significantly improve the performance of the development office? Is it worthwhile, imperative, or sensible to insist on campus-wide parent data integration if it negatively impacts the productivity of development or any of the other offices?

Many people assume that schoolwide data integration is easy. The solution, it is assumed, is for the entire school to use the same or an "integrated" database. Exactly what "integrated" means is not clear, nor is it clear who would manage this and which office or offices would be in charge. No one would seriously suggest that the admissions, development, and business offices be merged and the staffs combined. It is often suggested, however, that a relatively simple database choice could seamlessly let multiple offices share data and yet not corrupt or harm each other's records.

The dream is that a parent would be able to contact anyone, from the nurse to the development office to a teacher or coach, and all necessary information would be centrally available. Submitted changes would be input from any office, and everyone's reports, mailings, and directories, as well as the school's website, would be instantly updated. Regardless of the reality, parents often assume that this can be done.

This kind of integration has been attempted by colleges, the military, the FBI, and large corporations. Despite millions of dollars and years of planning and work, the results are generally disappointing. Rather than one central uniform system that satisfies all, the reality is that basic tasks are more difficult than before, and the ability to suggest or to enter corrections is reduced. The affected departments often export their data and return to working separately, ironically ignoring the "integrated" system.

For an individual school to truly integrate all functions would require years of planning and hundreds of thousands of dollars of custom programming. Even then, success would be far from certain. A more practical alternative is somewhere in the middle — using "best of breed" solutions for each office and coordinating when possible. Campus-wide coordination is best accomplished by naming a school database administrator and holding regular data coordination meetings with representatives of all affected offices.

TECHNOLOGY CHOICES AND TOTAL COST OF OWNERSHIP (TCO)

Given the threshold effects of technology, decisions about hardware, software, and other technologies can dramatically affect the productivity and effectiveness of the office overall. The cost of owning a database system and any technology should be evaluated on the basis of purchase price and setup as well as on the basis of possible loss of productivity and income if the technology is not installed. Being inefficient has a cost. Not staying in close and personal touch with constituents has a cost. What is not done may be significantly more costly than what is done, because solicitations from independent schools compete with all other solicitations that reach their constituents.

Given the emergence of new technologies, it is prudent to reevaluate technology systems every two to three years. When evaluating, look at the Total Cost of Ownership (TCO) — both tangible and intangible costs.

The tangible costs are the purchase price, training, yearly support, and setup. The more important intangibles are loss or gain of efficiency, productivity, and preparedness. If you save $3,000 by buying or keeping an older, unreliable car but are often late for work because of breakdowns, the savings are questionable. If you must also avoid long trips, visits to friends, weekends away, and driving at night, the minor cash savings have a significant intangible cost.

If the current database is hard to use or inflexible and the office produces far fewer mailings, cannot noodle, and must produce reports outside the system, the system is extremely costly on a daily basis. These costs are hard to quantify but could represent hundreds of thousands of dollars in lost donations. It is hard to justify not considering a change just because "we have already spent so much." Each day the old system remains, the intangible costs mount, quickly surpassing the replacement costs.

This is an exciting time of new opportunities. The challenges of reaching giving targets require everyone to be open to new options.

BEST PRACTICES
Technology and Philanthropy

Buy fewer computers each time, replacing a few each year. Do not skimp on basic hardware, but do not buy the highest end either. Do not buy homebuilt or generic computers. Purchases should be made within the context of a strategic plan.

Consider laptops rather than desktops because they are far more versatile overall. A stand-alone monitor can be used with a laptop for better viewing in the office.

Pay attention to the personal organizer, cell phone, GPS, and media player market. The landscape is changing rapidly. The ability to access e-mail and data while outside the office is a great convenience.

Be cautious about sales demos or conference presentations. The successful integration of a seemingly must-have new technology usually requires a combination of training, staffing, preparedness, and support. Those may be lacking at the school and add to the total cost of ownership (TCO). Consider a small trial implementation of a new gadget or web service.

Do not overburden the development office. When the development office is considered the office of record, tasks such as mailing labels for teachers, the school directory, and summer enrollment mailings may fall to the staff. This both overburdens the development office and unnecessarily delays those jobs for others.

Base the selection of a development office database first on functionality and productivity and the ability to support development tasks. Losing hundreds of hours of productivity in mailings, searches, and reporting in order to make updating the current family records easier schoolwide is not cost-effective. Each office should seek systems that make it productive. Data coordination should be viewed as a bonus rather than as a first criterion.

Organize a schoolwide data coordination working group. Data coordination is a person-to-person process that requires organization and leadership. Each school should have a forum or committee at which development, admission, registrar, guidance, and business professionals plan ways to share and to exchange information. Any school that believes its offices can remain uncooperative and solve conflicts with integrated software is not facing reality.

Strive to make communications friendly, timely, and easy to access. Offer an easy way to opt out. Users appreciate the option to unsubscribe from a mailing list, even if they do not exercise the option. They also appreciate a one-click sign-up or a one-click link to a well-organized, single web page.

CHAPTER 16

Soliciting the Major Gift

By Kathleen A. Kavanagh

Major donors give for a variety of reasons, including belief in a cause and a desire to make a difference. They also give because someone asked and, more often than not, because they were asked in person to consider a special gift that would have an impact on an institution or program that matters to them.

It would seem simple, then, for a school to build a strong major gifts program based on personal, face-to-face solicitations of those potential donors who have the greatest capacity to make a major gift. And at some schools, personal solicitation for major gifts is part of the fund-raising culture.

At many other schools, however, building a staff and volunteer program with a dedicated focus on personal solicitations remains a challenge. More than one volunteer has been heard to say, "I'll do anything but ask for money."

Increasingly, development and alumni staff members at independent schools work directly with potential major gift donors. However, whether the solicitor is a staff member or a volunteer, his or her job is to present a compelling giving opportunity to a potential donor. Potential donors deserve a thoughtful conversation about their values and how their gifts would advance the school's mission and goals.

Solicitors are at their best when they appreciate the philanthropic process. They must be donors themselves to understand the joy of giving and to appreciate the impact that gifts make on a school. A good solicitor wants to provide that same opportunity to others, is committed to the school's mission and the goals that will achieve that mission, and can articulate why giving matters.

PREPARING DONORS FOR MAJOR GIFTS

Although major gifts are defined differently at different schools, they most often start at a range of $25,000 to $100,000. Donors who have the capacity and inclination to make these gifts typically represent no more than 5 to 10 percent of the potential pool.

Major gifts are most often the result of a relationship with a prospective donor that school leaders, fellow donors, and volunteers have developed over time. Furthermore, with few exceptions, major gifts come from donors who have given in the past — most often, annual fund gifts. Even current parents at a secondary school, who have a relatively few years during which to become engaged beyond the usual parent activities, are likely to have some additional relationship with staff or leadership before they make a major gift. Alumni who make major gifts will often have spent years building relationships as donors and volunteers before making their first major gift. This engagement — beyond standard "cultivation" activities — is what can lead to a significant philanthropic investment in the school. The more prospective donors are involved in the life of the school and the more familiar they are with its mission and priorities, the more likely they are to want to give.

Before the solicitation of potential major gift donors can begin, it is important to be strategic about their involvement with the school by taking these steps:

- Identifying those who have both the capacity to make major gifts and a connection or interest in the school's mission

- Orchestrating their engagement with the school and its programs at both intellectual and emotional levels

- Generating a sense of "ownership" of the major gift objectives and pride in the past accomplishments of the school

- Building trust in the school's leadership as well as confidence in the quality of the program and the use of gifts in the way the donors intended

- Providing ongoing and thoughtful stewardship

- Ensuring that the solicitor can articulate a compelling case and can describe potential gifts that will have a significant positive effect on the school

INGREDIENTS OF A SUCCESSFUL
PERSONAL SOLICITATION

The major gift solicitation is almost always a process, rarely a single event. Still, there comes a stage in that process at which a specific conversation about the gift must take place.

The successful solicitation includes the preparation, the gift conversation, and the followup.

Preparation

The members of the solicitation team should carefully plan the conversation before they meet face-to-face with the prospective donor to discuss a specific goal and the philanthropic gift that will make that goal achievable. If the staff and solicitors are not sure which project or objective will be of greatest interest or how much to ask for, it is not yet time for the solicitation conversation. Additional cultivation is needed to fully engage the prospect and to get to know his or her interests and capacity.

The solicitation team should include the volunteers or staff members (or both) who are best able to present a compelling case and to explain to the donor how the gift would advance the school's mission. Social, intellectual, philanthropic, or financial peers of the prospective donor can play an important role in encouraging thoughtful consideration of a gift.

Solicitors should consider carefully the conversation they will have with a prospective donor. While a "script" rarely works, neither does improvisation. It is helpful for solicitors to consider questions and responses that a potential donor might present and to be ready with appropriate responses. It is also important that the team of solicitors agree in advance on assigned roles for each team member, especially which person will make the specific request for the gift.

Proposals should be tailored to meet the interests and gift capacity of the prospective donor. Requests based on past giving are almost never helpful; the request for a major gift should be designed to raise sights and to invite gifts that set a new standard for the school. The best case for the gift is rarely about the need for money but rather about the positive influence the donor can have on the school and its mission.

Respect for the potential donor involves careful consideration of the setting and timing of the gift conversation. If a spouse or partner should be part of the discussion, he or she should be included in the cultivation process as well as the solicitation. Social occasions or public places with no privacy are not appropriate settings for what should be a private, personal, and business-like discussion.

Donors don't appreciate being surprised by a solicitation. Whoever is making the appointment should ask permission to visit in order to discuss a gift. This conversation should not be the first encounter the solicitor has with the prospective donor. Ideally, he or she has been engaged in several conversations about the school, is knowledgeable about the issues and goals, and is ready to discuss a major gift.

The Gift Conversation

A good solicitor checks his or her nerves at the door and puts the prospective donor at ease. Staff and volunteers who have qualms should remember that the conversation is about the donors and their interests, not about the solicitor's discomfort. Phrases to avoid include, "I don't know how I got talked into doing this." Invite conversation that stays away from "yes" or "no" answers but, instead, helps the prospective donor discuss why he or she values the school today.

These topics should be addressed early in the gift conversation:

- The opportunity to help the school in significant ways, to solve a problem, to help close the gap between resources and opportunity

- The gift request: how much?

- The near-term impact of the gift: fulfilling an exciting opportunity or critical need, influencing other significant potential donors, ensuring momentum

- The long-term impact of the gift: institutional quality and reputation, building a legacy of philanthropic support

Be mindful that most prospective donors are interested in quality. They are reassured when they hear about current strengths and accomplishments of the school, its students, and its leadership.

A good solicitor stays focused and respects the time a prospective donor has set aside to discuss a gift to the school. A good solicitor is specific and talks about projects and not dollars. The prospect should be asked to join the solicitor by making a specific gift in order to achieve specific goals for the school.

Boldness counts for something in these conversations, so a good solicitor is not timid about the project or the requested gift amount. Discuss great dreams for the school and the specific ways in which major gifts serve the students, faculty, and program. Never hesitate to invite someone to join in that excitement and to make an extraordinary gift. Let the prospective donor decide what he or she wants to do — don't decide for him or her by assuming that the request is too large. A common fear of solicitors is that the prospective donor will ask, "What in the world possessed you to think that we could give that much money?" The answer: "We know that it will take leadership gifts to fulfill the school's dreams and we want to offer that opportunity to everyone who might consider making those gifts." If the solicitation is for a specific campaign, a gift table can be a helpful tool to show the kinds of gifts that will make the campaign a success.

Good solicitors know how to listen: It is important to let the prospective donor talk about his or her interests or ask questions. Listen actively and pause to think about the response. Objections are not necessarily a "no"; for example, the prospect might say, "That's a much larger gift than I was expecting to make." There is no "no" in that response, just a comment. Is it indeed a larger gift than he or she might have been considering? Will the prospect reflect on the impact he or she can make and consider that gift?

Present the case for support and the opportunity for leadership in a way that is clear, compelling, and without apology. Don't offer a pledge period if the donor doesn't need it. It is easy to preempt the decision by saying, "I know that is a lot of money, but you can pay it over five years" when in fact the donor is ready and able to make the gift now or over two or three years. Offer the pledge as a way to help the donor do what he or she wants to do — make the best gift.

Remember that an immediate decision is unlikely. The prospective donor has been asked for the thoughtful gift and will generally need time to give a thoughtful response. Be ready to offer options that can address concerns. For example, if the prospective donor says, "I'd like to do that but don't think I can, based on my current circumstances," the solicitor can discuss gifts of available assets as well as other gift vehicles and can suggest that a school representative would be happy to discuss those opportunities.

Confirm whatever decision or next step was made before leaving the meeting. Be responsible for the next step. Instead of saying, "Give me a call once you have time to think it over," suggest "I'll call you next week to find out if you have any questions." If another meeting is needed, suggest a date. If the prospective donor wants additional information, confirm that the appropriate material will be sent and follow up with a phone call. Or offer to bring the materials in person to a next meeting.

Be appreciative of the time and of the gift decision, if it is made. Successful solicitations leave an informed advocate for the mission and goals of the school and always leave the door open for future gifts.

Followup

The solicitation meeting should include specific steps for followup. The solicitor or solicitation team should identify clear next steps and remain proactive in seeking closure, whether a gift is made or the decision is "not now." Set a timetable for followup, which might include a revised proposal based on the gift conversation, additional meetings with the solicitation team or with others at the school, or information about gift options. Even when a prospective donor declines to give, the solicitor acquires valuable information that can guide future solicitations.

Followup extends beyond the gift decision; appropriate acknowledgment of the gift decision, documentation of the gift and its uses, gift recognition, and a good stewardship plan pave the way to future major gifts.

COMMON BARRIERS TO PERSONAL SOLICITATION

*"I hate to ask for money" or "I can't imagine how you do the work
you do [asking people for money]."*

Asking is not begging. Great schools have great missions, and they have
alumni, parents, and friends who give in support of those missions. The need
is real: Major gifts support students and faculty in extraordinary ways, and
donors enjoy a sense of lifelong pride and satisfaction when they make special gifts that help the school achieve its mission.

Conversations about giving are not begging for money (or shouldn't be).
The school didn't somehow mismanage its funds or do a bad job of budgeting. Instead, inviting individuals to make a major philanthropic commitment is about letting donors share in the school's vision.

Many volunteers who don't like to ask for money will say that they
don't like being rejected. It's easy to say that it isn't personal, but it feels
personal. No one, even the most seasoned fund-raising professional, finds
rejection easy.

However, the best fund raisers, staff and volunteers, know that people
enjoy making gifts and welcome the opportunity to play a leadership role
in the future of a school that matters to them. Those who have resources to
share appreciate the opportunity to talk in person about the school's mission and goals and to learn how they can positively influence the school's
future. Characterizing fund raising as a "task" diminishes the act of giving by
reducing it to a transaction, some kind of obligation to be endured. In fact,
the solicitor isn't asking for money; he or she is talking about giving and the
impact of gifts on the school's ability to fulfill its mission every day.

"I need more information before I can ask for the gift."

Major gifts are based on relationships, ideally between the prospective donor
and the school, and often between the prospective donor and a volunteer
or staff member. The best relationships — those that lead to a comfortable
conversation about giving — follow interactions and activities that provide
information that any solicitor should have about a potential donor:

- Does this individual have the capacity to make a major gift?

- Is there a particular area of interest — scholarships, endowment, facilities — that this donor is most likely to support?

- Is he or she charitable by nature? Is there evidence of previous giving to the school or to other charitable organizations?

It is tempting to delay a solicitation in search of more information. This search is often a comfort for the solicitor but, on scrutiny, does not add value to the solicitation. The search for "just some more information" can divert the solicitor from the focus of the personal solicitation: to provide an opportunity to discuss the school's mission and how a major gift from this prospective donor at this time will have a lasting impact on the school. Personal solicitation of major gifts is not conducted in "cold calls." The engagement process should include strategic steps that help the solicitor get to know prospective donors and their interests. No research profile can provide information that replaces what can be learned in interactions with prospective donors.

"This prospective donor needs more cultivation."

One of the more difficult decisions to make is when to put a formal proposal in front of a prospective donor. There have been cultivation and engagement activities. Were there enough? Is there one more action that would significantly change the potential donor's response to the proposed gift? If the answer is "yes," take that step.

At the same time, that "one more step" should not be a delay tactic. Today's prospective major gift donors are a relatively sophisticated group. Local and national organizations, colleges and graduate schools, and other independent schools may have asked for significant gifts or may be in the cultivation process. Too much cultivation and the failure to move deliberately toward a specific solicitation can lead prospective donors to question just why they continue to be invited to events and asked for personal meetings to discuss the school with no specific agenda in sight.

"I don't like to ask for a specific gift."

Good solicitors know that prospective donors want to have a positive effect on a program or objective that is of interest to them and that is a priority for the school. It is a courtesy to a prospective donor to come to the gift conversation prepared with a specific proposal that has been tailored to likely interests and capacity. The gift discussion should be about the program or project; at the same time, prospective donors need to know the kinds of gifts that will underwrite the program or project as well as set new standards of giving at the school. Talking about a specific gift, using examples of other gifts at that level and gift tables, helps the potential donor consider how he or she can have the greatest impact on the school.

CONCLUSION

Talking to prospective donors about major gifts need not be complicated. Here are some key points for a well-prepared major gift solicitation:

- Be a donor and appreciate the joy of giving.
- Rehearse the conversation and be prepared.
- Have a compelling case for support and articulate a personal commitment to its goals.
- Be forthright and direct about the impact of a gift on the school and its mission.
- Talk about a specific project or program and the specific gift request the prospective donor is being asked to consider.
- Listen and respond appropriately. Let the prospective donor talk about what he or she wants to do.
- Remember that "no" is often "not now," and "not that much" is not "no."
- Respect the donor's decision and say "thank you."
- Be clear about the next steps and be responsible for them.

Remember that gifts are made when people are invited to give and when they feel good about the impact that their philanthropy will have on current and future generations of students and teachers. Taking time to meet in person with potential donors, to discuss the school's goals, and to allow them to be part of the school's future in significant ways shows respect for their role as members of the school's community. Never underestimate the power of the personal conversation as a means of communicating the important role of philanthropy in sustaining the values the prospects share with the school.

CHAPTER 17

Writing for Development

By Helen A. Colson and Anne Seltzer

The best fund raisers write well. They know that literate communication from the development office is essential if they are to build and sustain relationships with prospects, donors, and volunteers.

Aren't students at independent schools taught that no cause can be advanced unless the advocate has a facility for language? How can parents and alumni expect anything less from those whose cause is their loyalty and support? How will potential donors regard an annual giving appeal that would receive a C– in their school's ninth-grade English class? Why should a major donor respond to a wordy, unspecific, and repetitive case for support?

Most development professionals are never told how much writing they will be doing and how important it will be. Yet many donors are reached primarily through the written word. They come to "know" the school through letters and e-mails from the development office. Therefore, every development office should include at least one skilled writer who can compose in many voices, including those of the head of school and the board chair.

GOOD WRITING IN A NUTSHELL

Good writing is simple, concrete, interesting, and understandable. It has a clear purpose, is well organized, and is appropriate for its audience.

The best fund raisers also understand the relevance of timing and tone:

- To persuade a prospect, they must write with clarity, warmth, and grace.

- To respond to a gift, they must write promptly, with sincerity and ease.

- To document a donor's request, they must write with precision and care.

SOME KEY POINTS

Here are some key points to consider in writing for development:

- *Do not cut and paste.* Taking a paragraph here and there from another fund-raising letter or foundation proposal rarely works. The text does not flow smoothly. It is far better to outline and write each document individually.

- *Avoid using adjectives like "creative," "innovative," and "unique."* Instead, vividly describe the project or the need so that its imaginative and in-dividual qualities clearly hop off the page. Strong verbs always trump overused adjectives.

- *Be consistent.* Keep pronouns consistently singular or plural within a sentence. Do not change the text at random from the third person ("the school") to the first person ("we") and then back again.

- *Be concise.* In particular, avoid repeating facts or ideas without ampli-fication or purpose.

- *Avoid using the passive voice.* Instead of saying, "Your gift will be ap-preciated," use the active voice ("We appreciate your gift.") Your copy will be more persuasive and compelling.

- *Proofread and proofread again.* Spell-checks are helpful, but they do not catch all spelling, grammatical, and punctuation errors. There is no substitute for careful reading and rereading of a final proposal by two different people.

- *Start well; end well.* While the entire written piece should be exemplary, take extra care in the beginning of a letter or proposal and find an especially appropriate way to conclude.

LEARNING TO WRITE

"I am fully confident when I speak, but when I try to write, I freeze."
Many development professionals who have excellent oral communication skills struggle to write. They speak with spontaneity and passion, but their writing is ponderous and verbose. There are some simple techniques to improve one's writing, but they all require a willingness to make good writing a priority.

A good writer:

- Imagines a live conversation with a favorite donor, especially the passion and persuasion that the writer would bring to the meeting. Then he or she writes it down with the same effectiveness.

- Asks a polished writer to give candid feedback on some writing samples.

- Schedules an hour with a favorite English or journalism teacher and edits some writing samples together.

- Understands basic grammar. Many donors, especially the older ones, will judge the writer and the school by the literacy of the writing.

- Conforms to conventional standards when writing a letter. This includes the correct placement of the date as well as an appropriate salutation and closing.

- Avoids clichés and overused adjectives such as "unique" and "excellent"; looks for more descriptive and fresher words.

- Saves and studies particularly effective written pieces.

- Avoids too many "I's" in letters and messages. Focuses on the recipient.

WRITING ON THE INTERNET

The web is now the primary communication tool for independent school constituents, young and old. It's hard to beat the timeliness and speed of an e-mail. But it's easy to find e-mails that are sloppy, loud, and verbose.

Writing on the web is different from writing for the printed page. The same rules apply, but there are some special temptations to avoid:

- Don't shout. Writing in CAPITAL LETTERS is not more persuasive.

- Don't overpunctuate and overemphasize to make a point. Avoid excessive exclamation points, asterisks, and quotation marks.

- Be careful with strong emotions in e-mails. Take the time to get the tone right.

- Avoid silly text messaging abbreviations such as "BRB" (be right back), "BTW" (by the way), or "TTYL" (talk to you later).

- Don't misspell. On the Internet, spelling counts more, not less.

- Don't write at great length just because it is so easy to do. Be simple and concise.

- Don't push the "send" button until you have reread your message.

A brief e-mail matters just as much as a long report. It creates a first and lasting impression. It may be the only chance to communicate. But remember: E-mail messages that are quickly sent and later regretted are never gone. Even if they have been deleted, they can always be retrieved from a computer's hard drive or the school's network backup system.

WRITING FOUNDATION GRANT PROPOSALS

A foundation proposal should represent a school accurately and well in every regard: the organization, the content, the presentation, the timing, and the appropriateness. Here are some tips for grant proposal writers:

- Research foundations carefully and thoroughly.

- Schedule a meeting with a foundation representative to discuss the proposal and to verify issues of timeliness and appropriateness.

- Collect sample proposals from several foundations and from other schools.

- Ask the potential foundation donor to send guidelines for applicants and an annual report.

- Follow the guidelines for applicants to the letter.

- Ask for a specific amount based on the school's need and the foundation's past giving history.

- Begin with a brief summary.

- Explain the project to be funded clearly and concisely.

- Verify all facts and statistics.

- Include a list of other foundations that have previously supported the school.

SOME SAMPLES: GOOD AND BAD

Consider these four sample letters on the following pages:

1. Letter A: A dull thank-you letter (page 192)
2. Letter B: A warm thank-you letter (page 193)
3. Letter C: A wordy, repetitious letter to alumni (page 194)
4. Letter D: A verbose letter to parents when a postcard would suffice (page 195)

Think about how the letters from Wanda Wonderful-Extraordinary (to which italics have been added) and William Gobblygook, each sent to large constituencies, reflect on the school, its leadership, and its development program. What grade would those letters receive in a high school English class?

THE POWER OF THE RIGHT WORDS

There are some pieces of writing that take exceptional care and thought, such as a school's reaction to a crisis or tragedy. These events, which call for a constituency-wide written response, have the potential to create community, to heal wounds, to offer comfort, to provide critical leadership, and to inspire.

It is always worth the effort it takes to craft such a letter even if must be sent during a time of crisis. Letter E on page 196, written by the new head of an East Coast boarding school in September 2001, illustrates the power of just the right words.

Good writing matters. The best development professionals take this task seriously. They take the time to write well and they can take pride in their product.

LETTER A:
A DULL THANK-YOU LETTER

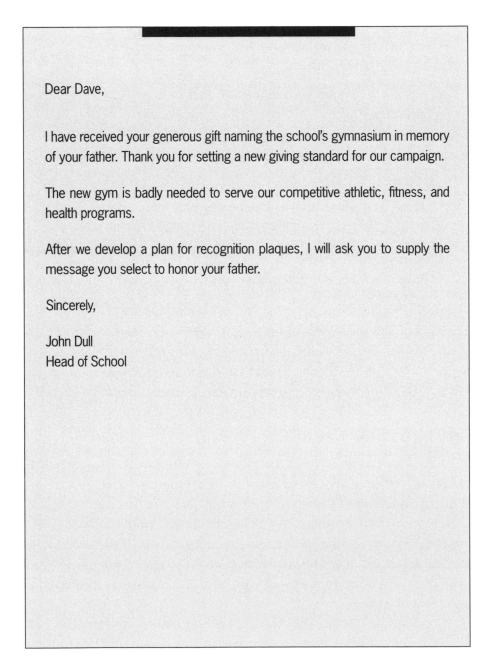

Dear Dave,

I have received your generous gift naming the school's gymnasium in memory of your father. Thank you for setting a new giving standard for our campaign.

The new gym is badly needed to serve our competitive athletic, fitness, and health programs.

After we develop a plan for recognition plaques, I will ask you to supply the message you select to honor your father.

Sincerely,

John Dull
Head of School

LETTER B:
A WARM THANK-YOU LETTER

Dear Dave,

My heart soared when I received your campaign pledge today. Our trustees will be excited and grateful to know that you wish to name our new gymnasium in memory of your father, Richard Smith.

Richard was both a fine athlete and a long-term generous supporter of our school. He understood that a balanced educational program includes athletics and that all students must be physically fit in order to learn. And he believed that athletics teaches students many of life's most important lessons. For all of these reasons, it seems particularly appropriate to honor your father's life in this way.

We are deeply grateful for your extraordinary contribution. I look forward to telling you in person how much your gift means to our school and how motivating it is to all who are working on the campaign.

Please rest assured that everyone who enters our gymnasium in the years to come will know that it bears Richard Smith's name, that we all loved and admired him, and that we share his conviction that athletics is a central component of a high quality education.

Sincerely,

John Warm
Head of School

LETTER C:
A WORDY, REPETITIOUS LETTER TO ALUMNI

Dear Alumni,

Many alumni from every decade in our history gathered at school on April 27 for a *wonderful* reunion. It was a pleasure to see so many alumni there and those who were not able to join us were sorely missed.

The *extraordinary* evening provided a *wonderful* opportunity to reminisce, see old friends, make new acquaintances, and learn about our latest campaign. Judging from the sentiments expressed, the school still means much to those who enjoyed the benefit of our *wonderful* education.

The evening was enhanced by the *extraordinary* participation of graduates on our fund-raising committee. We are so grateful for the *wonderful* commitment that so many alumni have made to the long-term health and prosperity of the school. It is *wonderful* to see the children here today, learning and growing in such *extraordinary* ways. We are pleased to give you a copy of our campaign video, which illustrates the *extraordinary* experiences so many alumni have had in the past.

Sincerely,

Wanda Wonderful-Extraordinary
Head of School

LETTER D:
A VERBOSE LETTER TO PARENTS WHEN
A POSTCARD WOULD SUFFICE

Dear Parents:

We have established a special phone communication system to provide
additional opportunities for parental input. During this year, we will give
added emphasis to the goal of communication and utilize a variety of
means to accomplish this goal. Your input, from the unique position as
a parent, helps us plan and implement an educational plan that meets
the needs of every child. An open dialogue, feedback, and sharing of
information between parents and teachers will enable us to work with your
child in the most effective manner.

Sincerely,

William Gobblygook
Head of School

LETTER E:
AN INSPIRING LETTER DURING A CRISIS

Dear Alumni, Parents, and Friends,

I am writing to share with you my perspective on the horrendous events of September 11th and the state of our school. I wish I could tell you that all the news about our immediate and extended family is good. Unfortunately, the father of two of our students is missing; the funeral for a 1994 alumnus was held this week. Needless to say, their families are especially in our thoughts and prayers.

Let me describe to you what I learned firsthand about our community this week. First, it is strong. I have witnessed countless examples of teachers and staff supporting students and even students supporting teachers. Within an hour of the first news, we assembled as a community to give a description of the facts as we knew them and to offer all students the following services:

- We opened up all offices and homes so that students could reach a telephone.

- We told them where our deans and counselor would be available to support them.

- We made available a big screen television where students could watch the news in the company of adults.

- We informed the entire community that the Chapel would remain open throughout the day.

- We asked students to attend class and deployed faculty with free periods to the residence hall common rooms.

- We offered students the opportunity to go home with their families if we had a record of their request and destination.

- We sent an e-mail to all parents with our plan of action.

We have reconvened several times since that first day. Perhaps one of the most moving events I have experienced came in the student-led prayer vigil around the flagpole. The first to offer a prayer for harmony and in support of the victims was a Muslim student. The diversity of our student body is a source of great strength and pride. Our school mission statement stresses tolerance and respect and concern for others. I have seen those traits in abundance.

Finally, I have learned quickly how supportive and compassionate this community is. Alumni have reached out to classmates in enormous numbers; parents have been incredibly helpful and communicative. Faculty, students, and staff have organized blood drives, funds, and other tangible ways of support. Faculty have used class time to help students understand the historical context of the events and to debate the next steps, thus helping our young people become informed citizens and responsible leaders of our future.

We also believe that we should provide for our students a shared intellectual experience around the many issues associated with this tragedy. To the extent that we can, in this busy place, we must educate ourselves and, at least, develop a common vocabulary of words and issues that are already under debate in the media. It may be as simple as a lesson in geography or as complicated as a lesson in politics, history, or religion. Finally, we also will work to emphasize that terrorism is a crime against humanity, and not just a crime against the United States, and as a diverse community representing 26 different countries, we can unite against what is happening around the world.

My thoughts and prayers are with all of you.

Warm regards,

John Goodleader
Head of School

ABOUT THE EDITOR

Helen A. Colson is president of Helen Colson Development Associates, a consulting firm serving independent schools. Previously, she worked as associate headmaster for development and planning at Sidwell Friends School. She is the author of the first two editions of *Philanthropy at Independent Schools* (NAIS) and the editor and a co-author of this text. She is a frequent speaker at NAIS and Council for Advancement and Support of Education conferences. You can reach her at *hcolson@hcda.com*.

ABOUT THE AUTHORS

Harold Brown has been director of alumni/ae affairs at Phillips Exeter Academy since 1991. He has served as a faculty member at the CASE Institute on Alumni Relations and as a member of the board of CASE International. You can reach him at *hbrown@exeter.edu*.

Carol Cheney is president of Cheney & Company, a communications firm that has served independent schools since 1983. She was the editor of and a contributing author to earlier NAIS marketing books and recently completed a term on the CASE Industry Advisory Council. She speaks frequently at national conferences. You can reach her at *ccheney@cheneyandco.com*.

Andrew Hamlin is in his 30th year in independent school advancement and in his 17th year as director of advancement at Princeton Day School. He has also served as director of development at The Lawrenceville School and as director of annual giving at St. Lawrence University. You can reach him at *ahamlin@pds.org*.

Ingrid Healy is director of advancement at The Parish Episcopal School. She has worked in a variety of independent school settings: boarding and day, elementary and pre-K through 12, single-sex, and coed. She is a frequent speaker at NAIS and CASE conferences. You can reach her at *ihealy@parishepiscopal.org*.

Jane Heimerdinger is director of institutional advancement at Iolani School. She previously worked as a teacher and school administrator. Jane is president of the Aloha Chapter of the Association of Fundraising Professionals and a board member of CASE, Western Division. You can reach her at *jheim@iolani.org*.

Leslie Hutchens is director of annual funds and major gifts at Sidwell Friends School. During the past 13 years, she has also worked at The Haverford School, the University of Richmond, and Hollins College. You can reach her at *hutchensl@sidwell.edu*.

Kathleen A. Kavanagh has served as senior executive vice president and marketing director at Grenzebach Glier and Associates since 1995. Previously, she led development programs at Vassar College, The Madeira School, Dana Hall School, and The Walters Art Museum. She speaks frequently at national conferences. You can reach her at *kakavanagh@grenzebachglier.com*.

Lucy E. Leitzell retired in 2008 after 30 years in independent school development at St. Thomas School, Sidwell Friends School, Lakeside School, and The Bush School. You can reach her at *lucyleitzell@yahoo.com*.

Carrie Levenson-Wahl is director of external affairs at the International School of Paris, where she began the school's fund-raising program eight years ago after a 20-year career in U.S. independent schools. She also consults with schools in Europe and Asia. You can reach her at *clwparis@gmail.com*.

Kevin J. McAllister created inRESONANCE, a technology firm providing consulting services for schools, in 1999. Previously he worked for 16 years at The Loomis Chaffee School and other boarding schools as technology director and as a teacher. You can reach him at *kevin@inresonance.com*.

Peter D. Relic is a former president of NAIS. He has spent 50 years in precollegiate education as a teacher at the Hawken School, as a principal, as a school head, and as a superintendent. You can reach him at *pdrelic@yahoo.com*.

Tracy G. Savage has been a senior consultant with Marts & Lundy since 2002. She also worked for 13 years as assistant head of school for advancement at the National Cathedral School. Tracy has co-authored several books on educational fund raising, including CASE's *Handbook of Institutional Advancement* (2000). She is a frequent speaker at national conferences. You can reach her at *savage@martsandlundy.com*.

Kathy Schulte is associate director of advancement at Princeton Day School. She has also served as director of development at the New Jersey SEEDS program and as admission director for Teach for America. You can reach her at *kschulte@pds.org*.

Anne Seltzer retired from The Peddie School in 2003 after working for 25 years as chair of the English Department, acting head of school, dean of faculty, and director of development. She now consults on fund raising and strategic planning. You can reach her at *aseltzer@seltzerrees.com*.

Herbert P. Soles is assistant headmaster for development at Norfolk Academy. Previously, he headed development programs at St. Stephen's School, Flint Hill School, St. Albans School, and Saint Andrew's School. He speaks frequently at CASE conferences. You can reach him at *hsoles@norfolkacademy.org*.